CHORONZON

VOLUME 1, EDITION 1

MARTINET PRESS

CHORONZON
VOLUME 1, EDITION 1
OCTOBER 2015

ISBN-13: 978-0692548127

ISBN-10: 0692548122

COVER ART and ATU III (p.84) by JOEL HRAFNSSON

TABLE OF CONTENTS

EDITOR'S FOREWORD

"AT MARTINET PRESS, WE CONCERN OURSELVES WITH PUBLISHING TEXTS THAT REFLECT THE DARKNESS THAT IS ENDEMIC TO REAL ANTINOMIAN SPIRITUALITY. IN THIS WE ARE UNAPOLOGETIC, AND REMAIN COMMITTED TO MAKING AVAILABLE TEXTS THAT INSTRUCT, RATHER THAN ENTERTAIN."

Shortly before launching Martinet Press, we asked ourselves whether the world needed yet another publishing house dedicated to Left Hand Path. After all, there are several commercial presses that have a fulltime owner/operator which produce very nice (if expensive) grimoires and talismans. Some of the presses have developed a very successful business model, and manage to find and promote aspiring occult authors. The publishers offer to publish the aspiring author's book and to locate an esoteric artist to design whatever summoning circles and sigils needed to bring the book "alive". The author makes a little cash, the artist gets a little more cash, the publisher makes a very tidy sum, and the readers obtain books that look and feel very nice after spending several hundred euros a copy.

Of course, no one wants to feel that they have paid hundreds of euros for "just a book", and so in the last decade the occult publishers began to use a different line of attack. You weren't paying hundreds of dollars for a book – you were buying an "awakened" text, a sacred talisman. The aspiring author would personally sign and sigilize your book, which was individually numbered so you knew you had a precious commodity. Some presses insisted that each book was "consecrated", and that by spending hundreds of euros, you were really buying a gateway to gnosis. Possession of the book was

seen as a mark of authentic spirituality, and in fact, in order to enter some secret lodges or temples, you needed to have purchased one or more of their consecrated texts. Of course, this sounds marvelous, especially if you're the publisher who makes a living off the work of other authors.

Some people will wisely point out that even if the content of such books is mediocre, then surely the occult art and the personal blood-inked sigil of the author gives the book a certain status. The term "talisman" and "consecration" is used liberally, as though these books are indeed some kind of treasure. But this is equally foolish. Look, let us take a respected painter like Richard Moult. If Moult does an original painting, we will all agree that it is high quality, and we might pay a lot of money to own a Richard Moult original. Thousands, maybe more. We know that Moult incorporates sigils into his painting, and so we might even think of his work as having a sacred character, as a real talisman of some kind. If he signs the painting in blood, we will really treasure it, it would be truly priceless.

But, what would happen if Moult has replicas made of his original painting? Are the replicas worth as much? Maybe it depends; if he were to recreate the paintings *by his hand alone*, that would be something. But if a machine or even another artist makes the replicas, then they are clearly not the same value or esoteric potency of the original image. Even if the replicas are printed in the highest quality, and even then if the artist signs in his own blood, they will still only be replicas of a great work. Even if Moult performed a grand ritual to consecrate the painting, he knows – and the publisher knows too – that those are just replicas of a real treasure.

So this is why, with all respect, we appreciate the craftsmanship of the most occult grimoires, but we cannot endorse people paying hundreds of dollars for texts that are being sold as "talismanic" or "exalted" or "enriched", or whatever other language that a clever publisher uses as marketing. Period. End of story.

But to return to our original question: so why another occult press, and what could we possibly bring to the table? What would distinguish Martinet Press from the other LHP publishing houses?

Eventually, we decided on three things that would define our Press: **content, coherence**, and **clarity**.

First, we believe in providing high quality **Content** to our readers. We only print authentic content, and insist on publishing only those authors who represent a genuine spiritual tradition, rather than creative fiction. People buy books on the occult because they are genuinely searching for spiritual experiences, and they often lack direct access to a living tradition that can provide them with the kind of instruction that they need in order to feel like they are making progress. This problem is doubly hard for those few occultists who feel an instinctive pull towards the world's darker spiritual traditions. Equally problematic is that many of the few sorcerers and priests who have wisdom to share will simply not publish with a big business esoteric publisher, because they're not interested in making money, or lining a publisher's wallet with the knowledge of their ancient traditions. Martinet Press works to find those rare authors in antinomian traditions, and offers to connect them to their potential students through the production of printed manuscripts. Authors don't have to be great writers, but they do need to demonstrate knowledge of a real spiritual tradition. Too many modern books purport to represent an "ancient knowledge", but are simply a cut-and-paste of other traditions or books on the market. To be valuable, *content needs to be valid and transformative.* When our intake editors read a genuine manuscript, it possesses a real energy, a vibrancy that is apparent. If a manuscript reads well, but has no power, it is not for Martinet Press. We believe in promoting quality content, and only quality content. A quality book gives you a vision of the tradition, and some basic idea on how to begin to practice it, and how to connect with the living current.

Second, we believe in **Coherence**. Many spiritual teachers have excellent communication skills, but have never written anything longer than a few pages. Martinet Press works with its authors to help visualize a book and give it structure. This means paying attention to the order of its content, the grammar, the spelling, the layout, and the overall language of the book. Not all of our manuscripts are submitted in English, and so translation may need to be arranged. For example, the *Devil's Quran* and *The Black Path* were translated from Arabic and French respectively, and so the Press takes care of such details in collaboration with the authors. Most of the texts need substantial editing, and this is not an easy process. We are working this year and next to expand our circle of artist allies, so that future editions have better illustration when it is called for in the manuscript.

Third, Martinet Press is very serious about **Clarity**. We are not interested in smoke and mirrors, "hidden" or "closed" orders, or anonymous and invisible authors with no public presence. Our authors (if living) are required to post their contact information in their works, and to make some effort at answering questions from readers. Equally important, we are largely a volunteer operation. Costs are kept at an absolute minimum, and neither the authors, the editors, or the artists receive anything more than a modest honorarium. The proceeds of the sales go back into buying review and contributor copies for authors and artists, for proofreading, and to cover what limited promotion the Press wishes to engage in. We do not sell talismans or ritual products called for in our books, as that is tantamount to profiteering. Last, we do not believe in giving false hopes to our readers – the occult is not a get-rich-quick scheme, and the overwhelming number of occultists are seeking escapism. Spiritual evolution is hard, and dark spiritual evolution is very dangerous. Most "Satanists" are really more akin to gothic neopagans: they just want a spiritual path that requires absolutely no spiritual discipline or sacrifice, and spend a lot of time trying to convince people that they're really dark and scary. Real Satanists (if you ever meet one) are really terrifying people, whose spiritual disciplines have so warped their humanity that they genuinely need to work hard to blend in. There is a great difference, yet many people will easily confuse the two. We seek to bring Clarity to our readership, and help to distinguish the true from the false (if not the good from the bad). One of the things we have realized is that there are many sinister artists and authors, who represent a spiritual tradition that we want to support, but may not be in a position to publish an entire book. The *Choronzon* journal is intended to showcase those individuals and traditions, and is our way of supporting the work that they're doing. We believe absolutely and unreservedly in the exaltation of Darkness, but we also know that the dark gods take different forms and speak with different voices to many initiates. We believe that the work under this cover is indicative of the diversity of genuine occult tradition, be it through the artist's brush or the author's pen.

We hope you enjoy this edition of *Choronzon*. There is a great store of esoteric talent and information contained in these pages, and we are genuinely proud to have such a range of collaborators and contributors. Looking forward to hearing your own feedback, if you have a mind to share.

❖ **The Editorial Team at Martinet Press**

STACK THE BODIES TO GOD

CZAR AZAG-KALA, TEMPEL OV BLOOD

As the sun slowly began to set across the autumnal fields, the few large oaks setting close to the small dwelling blocked the last vestiges of the orange light so that the shadows darkened in the little room as Gwydion sat naked, cross-legged, upon his bed. The black comforter beneath him was old, weathered and encrusted with filth, having never been washed during the more than a decade since it had been in his possession. The sheets beneath it were in an even more dire condition, nearly dry-rotted, but with their dirt carefully brushed away - at least in part - each night before sleep.

That said, however, more often than not sleep came not during the night but during the day - Gwydion's existence having become mostly nocturnal during these last three to four years except in those necessary times when he had to conduct some small business during daylight hours to keep himself afloat according to passable operative standards, body and mind together and with a functional, if utilitarian, infrastructure. His many, many years of highly subversive activities up to and including fallback from the same - sometimes catastrophic in nature - had engendered in him use of his own wiles to maintain his own survival via somewhat creative means - quite austere though it would seem from the lens of the bourgeoisie - but which facilitated minimal contact with the outside world whilst maintaining maximum aggression and functionality as a command center for his far-flung hive.

A painful howl ripped its way through the erstwhile twilight silence and a disturbing grin spread across Gwydion's face. The dogs there in the old farms surrounding his squalid residence at this time, like clockwork, would begin to ascertain on a subtle level those many horrific shades which would begin to rise up from various clandestine shrines and points of inter dimensional compromise during that juncture when the veil between the gross and subtle worlds became thin.

By the time the country was ensconced in proper dark, every dog for a quarter mile circumference would be howling blood lust and frothing at the mouth, their old-timer Christian owners never quite getting used to what had gotten into them despite the fact that the scenario repeated itself night after agonizing night.

In time the sounds would be drowned out by the myriad of night birds, the insects and, during the rains of summer, the frogs - but these later would join in cacophony not by dint of threat, as did the domestic beasts and their decidedly puerile domestic owners, but rather as a herald of nocturnal welcome amidst brethren, for they too lived in, and for, the night energies and all that such entailed and often, demanded.

Gwydion sat upon the bed, naked, and watched as the dwindling orange-hued light began to descend into the fullness of night. As that light receded, another light began to glow slowly but steadily from the tetrahedron which sat upon a plinth in front of him in a bluish hue, illuminating a large image tacked to the wall above, its edges frayed with age and use – having been carried with him, along with the tetrahedron, from staging area to staging area over the many years.

Gwydion smiled, with unabashed sinister exultation, as he considered those bastard, baying dogs without and those horrific shades which drew themselves up, night after night, from the damp, sour earth surrounding his inflexion. For each one of them, he knew – in each spot – a deed of darkness done, an act of evil performed. Not simply in a ritual manner, nay, for Gwydion knew – as did his followers – that it was only hardcore evil, evil in the real-world – with real victims and the potential real consequences for those so enacting which drew forth the Dark Forces from beyond the Abyss.

As he ruminated upon these matters and the veritable web that surrounded his residence – the core lair from which extended other lairs like it, amidst their principalities and other geographic divisions the tradition of so ordering which he had carried down from his own initiation into the underground cultus of black vampirism (the nomenclature of *black* denoting a completely amoral posture) – he noticed that the bluish light from the tetrahedron began to emit a fractured light – a disturbance, a sign – a warning.

In concert he heard the sound of a slight mechanical buzzing from the corner of the room and – stretching himself up and out of the bed – proceeding to where a cellular phone, long out-of-date according to most standards and a burner to boot – assigned to another person, in another state and purchased from the barred window of a grimy five-and-dime in a metropolitan area – sounded its banal alarm.

Ah, a simple message relayed via small twinkling text – coded – but comprehensible for those in the know, in this case, him only. An operation by one of the nastier elements amidst his coterie was underway – and – as somewhere hundreds of miles away but within the continent of his residence an innocent began to orient themselves to innocence lost, a new life – or, perhaps – a living death, amidst those who designated themselves as inhabiting a state of undeath – so did the nocturnal creatures outside in the black country night begin to roar, so did the tetrahedron beneath the banner of that bane of all children and piety begin to pulsate with its horrific, bluish light – ever-fractured, ever seeking that greater harvest.

GNOSIS OF THE DEVIL

FRATER KAFYRFOS

DEVIL

Fundamentally Diabolic Gnosticism is comprised of Diabolism and Gnosticism. Gnosticism denotes a particular way of knowing, coming to know, and a path of knowledge. Diabolism in its crudest form pertains to the Devil, diabolic idolatry and devil worship. Diabolic Gnosticism thus explicitly means a way of knowing, coming to know, or knowledge of, the Devil. Diabolic Gnosticism is based on the concept of the Gnosis of the Devil, an occult or hidden knowledge attained by coming to know the Will of the Devil, and overcoming it, and also a certain way of being to come to know. The Will of the Devil is recognised by means of Devil Worship, rituals and individually targeted trials and ordeals that focus on challenging an individual physically, psychologically, spiritually and morally. One of the initial spiritual missions of Diabolic Gnosticism is to accept the Flesh, bound by the Black Sun, devoted unto the Devil (and the bestial, subhuman parts of us), but also achieve spiritual liberation within, upon and beyond this world. The Devil is a dark emanation of the Earth, and it is worldly. It is misanthropic and largely driven by the Will to Hate (or Loathe over Will). One becomes an open vessel poised to empathetically convey the Aphotic essence of the Devil and its sinister nature, as an unbeliever reconciles itself with the utility of holding and overcoming certain Diabolical beliefs.

BLACK SUN

The Black Sun is a powerful symbol of the potential within one's Blood. One manifestation of it holds within it the Sig Rune, the Trisigil and the Swastika. It is as the alchemical Nigra Sol and the Shadow of and over the undifferentiated Blood. By the Black Light of the Black Sun those who are endowed with the hidden divinity of the Blood are guided and urged to cleanse their impure Blood. It is by striving under the Black Sun that one becomes known and comes to know in proportion to their striving efforts. Thus the Black Sun represents Twelve Victories that are unique to each individual, yet must be achieved.

BLOOD

Pure Blood worship is part of Diabolic Gnostic Devil worship. The Devil is initially viewed and perceived as burning, being and existing within our Blood. We offer the impure elements of our blessed Blood and the impure Blood of our enemies unto the Devil. According to Diabolic Gnosticism the Will is deep within our Blood (or the Blood of the elect), as the Blood contains within it a portion of the Great External Chaos (also called Entropy) which is imbued with Acausality and Synchronicity. The Blood also contains within it the seeds of our biological imperatives, the psychological Shadow, our racial memory, our evolution and the paradox of causality contra acausality. It is through the Blood that we come to perceive (spiritually), as it is in the Blood that our potential lies –be it biological potential, spiritual potential, or portions of Chaos and Void. The rituals and ordeals of Diabolic Gnosticism are aimed at hearing the inner Will, and challenging Belief in all of its forms, to cleanse the Blood of Perception.

SATAN

The Satanic element of Diabolic Gnosticism revolves around the idea of Satan as the active element of antibelief, that which actively seeks values, morals and beliefs and opposes, challenges or destroys them. Satan is the Devil Worshipper purged of Belief, and the holocaustic Fires of the Swastika that cleanses the impurities of the Blood. Satan and the Swastika move to and fro about the Earth in a continual conflagration of fiery overcoming and progressive evolution. Satan is the existential being becoming, and the philosophical wanderer that tempers the utter hatred and malevolence of the undifferentiated belief driven Devil.

CHAOS

In place of the more commonly known Gnostic cosmology, Diabolic Gnosticism features a Noncosmology whereby all things are possible because of the overarching principle of the Great External Chaos. The Great External Chaos, or Chaos generally, had within it the potential to form the Cosmos and Universe from the Noncosmic. All things are emanated from Chaos because it was possible for them to be. That which is impossible does not come into being or existence. We cannot contemplate that which is impossible, because we view thoughts, dreams and fantasies as possible variations and emanations of Chaos. As such Chaos is knowable in part but unknowable in its totality. The Gnosticism of Diabolism recognises the Great External Chaos above and the portion of that same Chaos within each individual. Not all humans are viewed to be blessed with inner Chaos, as some have had their internal Chaotic flames doused with dirt, and void fills their souls. With this understanding all things become possible to those who do not believe.

UNBELIEF

Technically speaking, the Great External Chaos is a sychro-a/gnostic concept, meaning we neither believe nor do not believe in it absolutely. Instead we actively unbelieve in the Great External Chaos. Despite the unbelief in the Great External Chaos beyond all else, we accept it agnostically because of its pervading Synchronicity and the fundamental weaknesses inherent in the psychology of being human, such as our Will to Believe. The unbelief in Chaos is essentially a paradox. Diabolic Gnostics view the Great External Chaos as being and nonbeing, all things and nothing at once (and at no time). We aim to reconcile ourselves with this major source of potential energy to draw upon it and utilise it as per the Devil's Will, or be torn apart by it, as is the wont of Chaos.

BECOMING DIABOLIC GNOSTIC

Experience has shown us that our all-too-human needs have to be met before we can effectively harness this omnipotent chaotic energy. We have structured programs that develop discipline and self-awareness through physical, cognitive and psychological challenges. We focus on studying the three key domains of Psychology, Philosophy and Spirituality. We engage in strenuous trials that test our Will to Power, to achieve distant and difficult goals. As such our foundations become unbreakably strong and we can approach the Chaos A/Gnosis and the Diabolic Gnosis thereof with an understanding of deep and profound intention. The Path of the Devil is definitely not for everyone. An individual may be associated with Diabolic Gnosticism by engaging with our works and practices, or by identifying as a Diabolic Gnostic. There is no need to be an initiated member of Ecclesia Diabolica Gnostica (EDG) or the Order of Havayoth to be Diabolic Gnostic, and other orders may regard themselves as being Diabolic Gnostic. The key idea of the 'Order of Havayoth' is to 'Obey the Infernal Will of the Devil'. Let it be known! We rigorously screen potential members to EDG through psychological and physical testing for a minimum of 7 months before an application for Aphotic initiation is considered.

DIABOLIC GNOSTIC RITE OF SELF INITIATION: APHOS

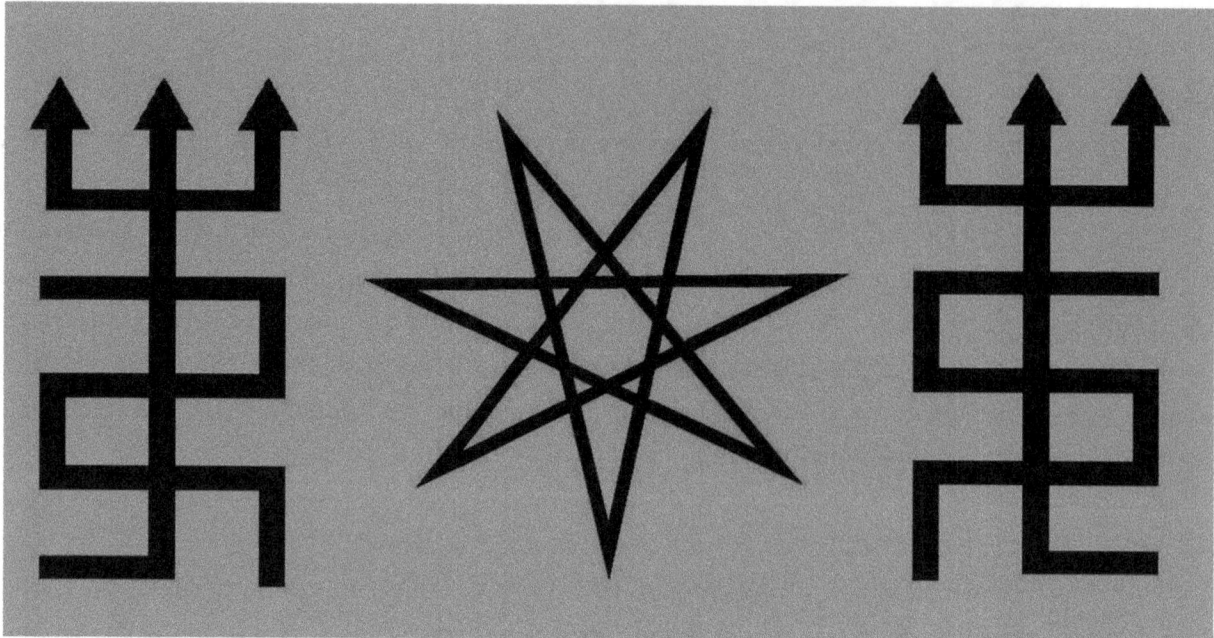

(Astral Seal of Aphos)

Requirements:

- Seven candles
- Ritual knife
- Anointing oil
- Incense
- Censer
- Black Candle
- Seven stones (optional)
- Astral Seal of Aphos painted on cloth or canvas

Location:

The Diabolic Gnosis Rite of Self Initiation: Aphos should be completed on a New Moon, outdoors in a secluded place on a cliff or beach facing tumultuous seas, on a mountain top, in a cave or cavern, in an old cemetery, an abandoned building (church, bunker, asylum etc.) or by a river, a lake, crossroads or an abandoned mine. The location has to exude energy or have special meaning to the potential initiate.

EXECUTION:

Preparation:

Place seven anointed candles in a circular shape to mark out a ritual space. These represent the Seven Points of Phosphorosophia and the Septagram, and they link the physical space to internal and external space. Each candle should be inscribed with the Seven Points of Phosophorosophia (Will, Creativity, Self, Strength, Usurpation, Unbelief, Wisdom). Depending on the location of the Rite of Initiation seven stones can also be placed around the ritual space with the candles positioned on top of them. As each candle is lit say 'Lucifer Illuminatio Mea!' and visualise a Sig Rune in the flame.

The ritual space can also be surrounded by branches of wormwood (or similar plants).

Set up a small altar on the ground using the Astral Seal of Aphos as the altar. A lone Black candle can be used to weight down the seal. Place the ritual knife to the right of the altar and the censer to the left.

Light incense (top up incense throughout the rite as required/desired).

Rite Proper:

Complete a HVHY Banishing Ritual

1. With your left arm stretched towards the centre of your ritual space and your right arm stretched outwards, walk widdershins around the ritual space, dragging up the energy with your right hand and chanting 'He Vau He Yod' during each rotation of the space. Your arms and body should form a Fyrfos as you move. Complete this seven times. Finish by standing and facing the Astral Seal of Aphos.

Complete a chakral meditation.

2. Place both hands over your Base (Will) chakral and seven times vibrate:

'Ur'

3. Then once exclaim:

"Via Diabolic Gnosis we come to know the true Will of the Devil, HVHY."

4. Place both hands over your Sacral (Individuality) chakra and seven times vibrate:

'Oh'

5. Then once exclaim:

"As Life Blood and Fire I am come of the Devil."

6. Place both hands over your Solar Plexus (Strength) chakra and seven times vibrate:

'Oo'

7. Then once exclaim:

"As Sun Fire in the Blood I blaze with Strength."

8. Place both hands over your Heart (Usurpation) chakra and seven times vibrate:

'Ah'

9. Then once exclaim:

"I cast the Blood unto the Fire and douse the Fire with Blood."

10. Place both hands over your Throat (Creativity) chakra and seven times vibrate:

'Ay'

11. Then once exclaim:

"I destroy and from utter destruction I create my own reality."

12. Place both hands over your Brow (Unbelief) chakra and seven times vibrate:

'Ey'

13. Then once exclaim:

"*Void of belief I perceive things as they are.*"

14. Place both hands over your Crown (Wisdom) chakra and seven times vibrate:

'*Ei'*

15. Then once exclaim:

"*Actively I come to know that which is unknown and knowable.*"

Contemplation of the Astral Seal of Aphos

16. Once the chakral chant is complete sit in the cross legged meditative pose in front the Astral Seal of Aphos, with both hands turned upwards. Then exclaim:

'*From the false light of the cursed Demiurge I am come unto the Way of Phosphorosophia. As Aphos void of Sof I am come. By the Seven Fires that enlighten this place I seek to find Phos and Sophia within, on and beyond this world.*'

The Sig Rune Anointing

17. Draw a Sig Rune on your brow with the anointing oil saying 'Hail Sig'. Smell the oil and feel it on your brow. Feel your Third Eye opening up.

Extinguishing Light of Sof

18. Move to each candle and sit or kneel in front of it. Focus on the light for a few moments, contemplate each of the Seven Points of Phosphorosophia (say them under your breath like a mantra if so desired), and then blow out each candle keeping the idea in your mind as the flame is extinguished. Perceive the increasing darkness as each candle is blown out, but feel the link between the energies of all of the candle points.

The Aphos Dedication

19. Return to the sitting stance in front of the Astral Seal of Aphos. Raise your arms up in the Sign of Apophis/Typhon and exclaim:

> 'As Aphos void of Sof I am come. I am come as a vessel filled with darkness, enthusiasm and potential seeking to fill myself with Diabolic Gnosis. It is my Will to dedicate my body, soul and mind unto the Path of the Devil. I offer my dedication, devotion and passion to Diabolic Gnosticism.'

The Aphos Blood Offering

20. With your right hand pickup the ritual knife and cut your left hand. Use the blood to draw a V under the Septagram on the Astral Seal of Aphos, and an X over the Septagram. Contemplate the meaning of the X as Blood being carried by the V as a chalice.

Slowly chant 'Aphos' (Ay-Fos) seven times.

Aphotic Meditation

21. Blow out the Black Candle, burn all of the remaining incense and meditate in the dark, focusing on the smells, sounds and images that you see to conclude the initiation.

Successful Initiation into the Ecclesia Diabolica Gnostica

Before conducting this rite it is best advised to contact the Ecclesia Diabolica Gnostica (EDG) (ecclesiadiabolicgnostica@gmail.com) to make us aware of your intentions. Self-initiation shows empathy with our Way, the Path of the Devil and Diabolic Gnosticism generally. To be considered for initiation into EDG a candidate will have to complete the Rite of Self Initiation: Aphos over 7 successive New Moons, and become physically prepared to complete the Marsttarial trial. On the day/night of assessment by one or more of our members, the candidate will have to organise, host and conduct an eighth Rite of Initiation: Aphos in the presence of the EDG representative/s, as well as the Oath of Secrecy and the Marsttarial trial.

VLF LABORATORIES

ATTO 631

V.L.F. Laboratories is the video section of the Current Q.309.

All pictures by Marco Malattia.

All concept by Rev. Ajin Ra'ah.

0

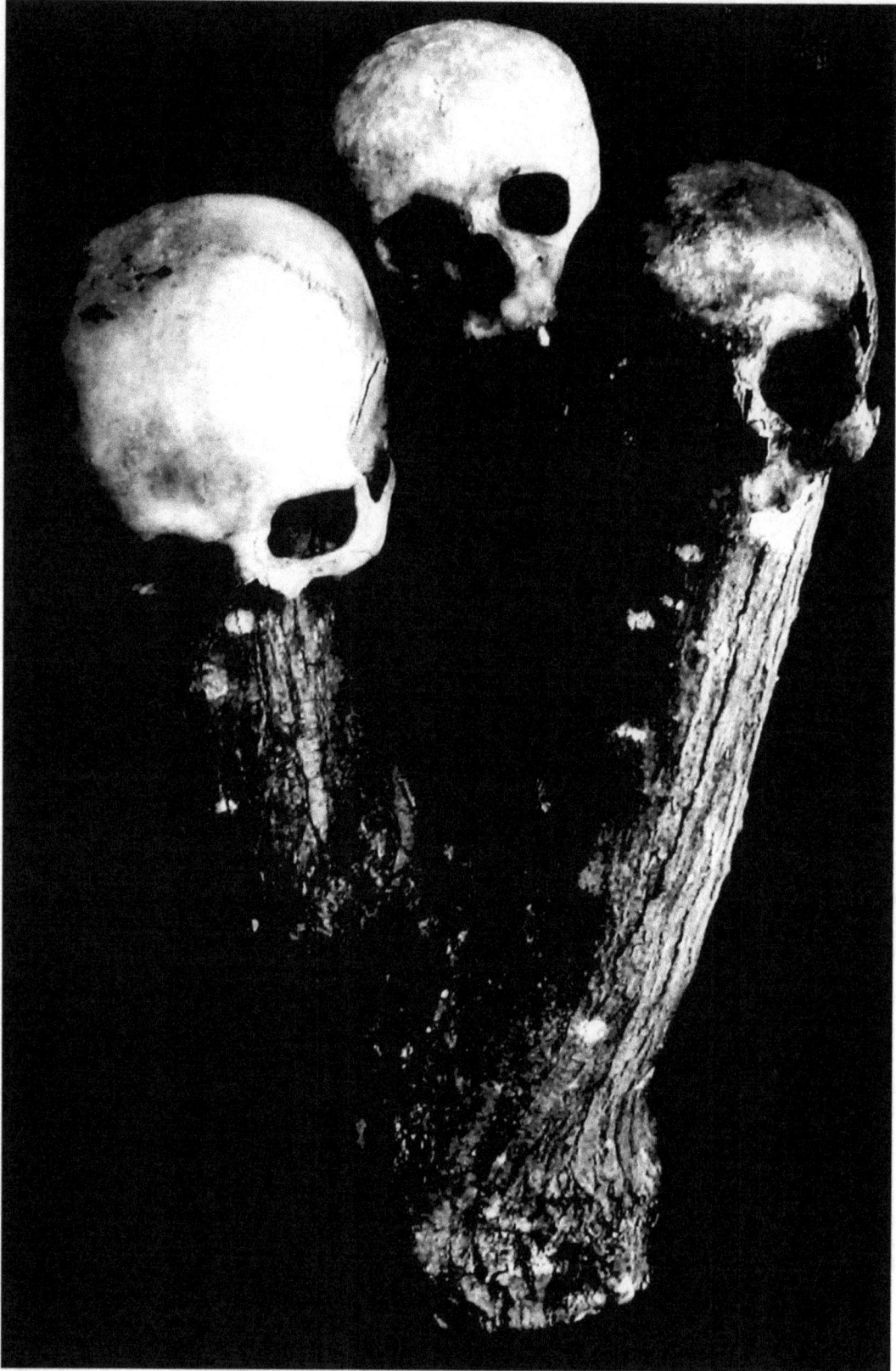

OO

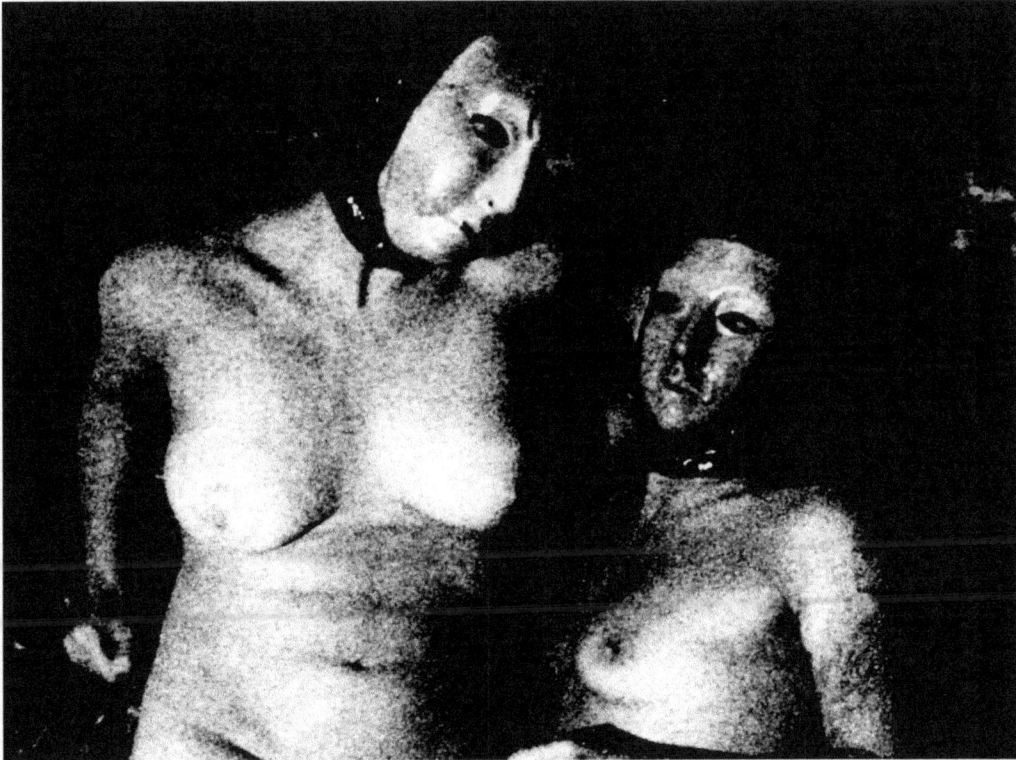

01

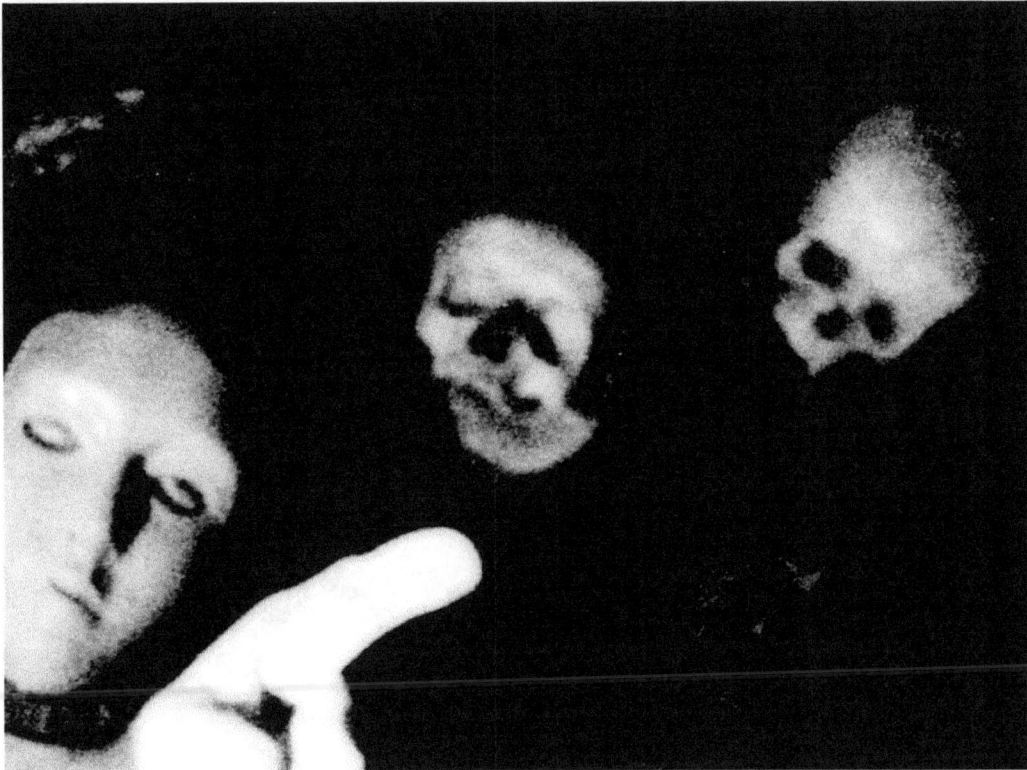

02

03

04

05

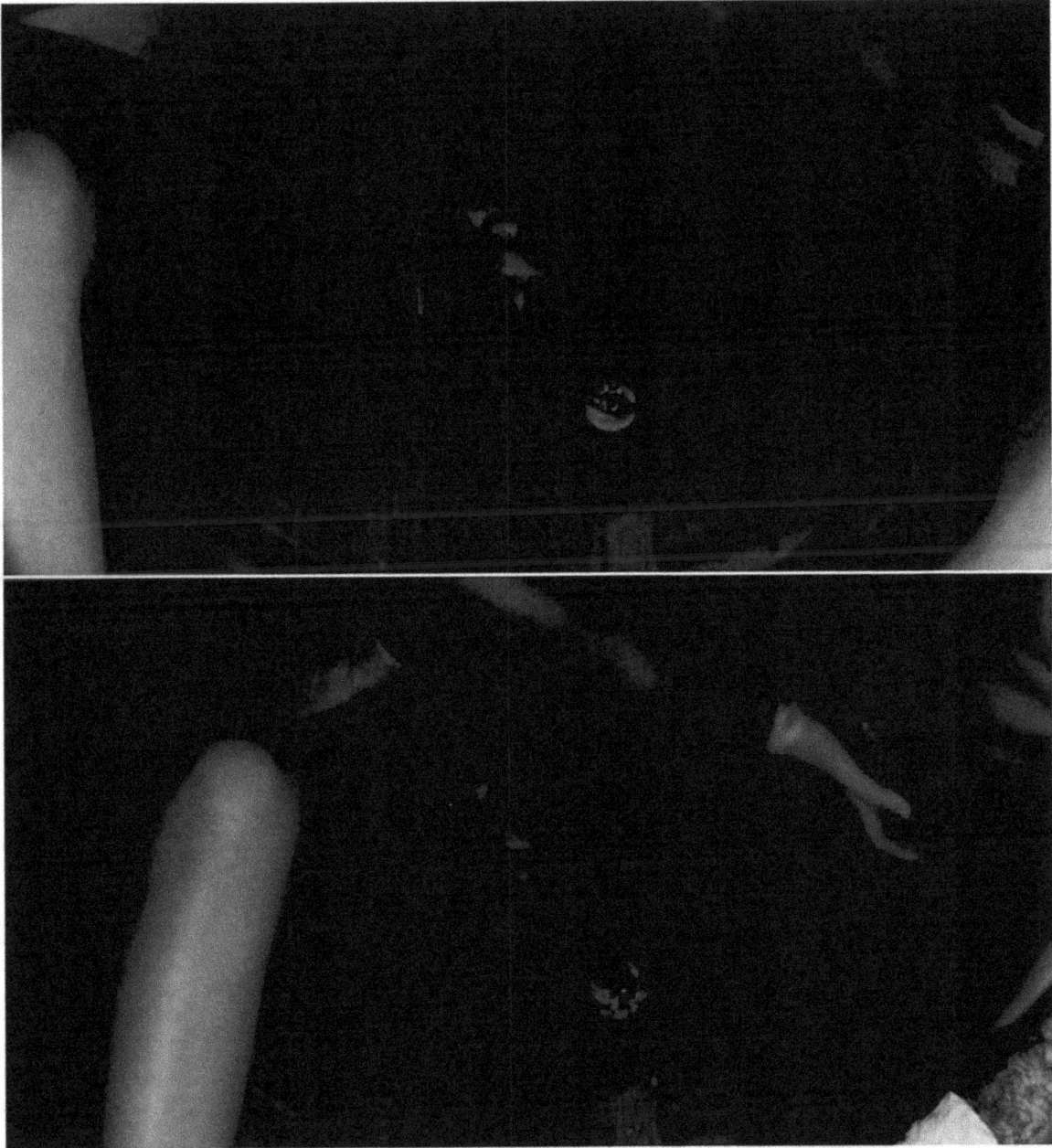

06

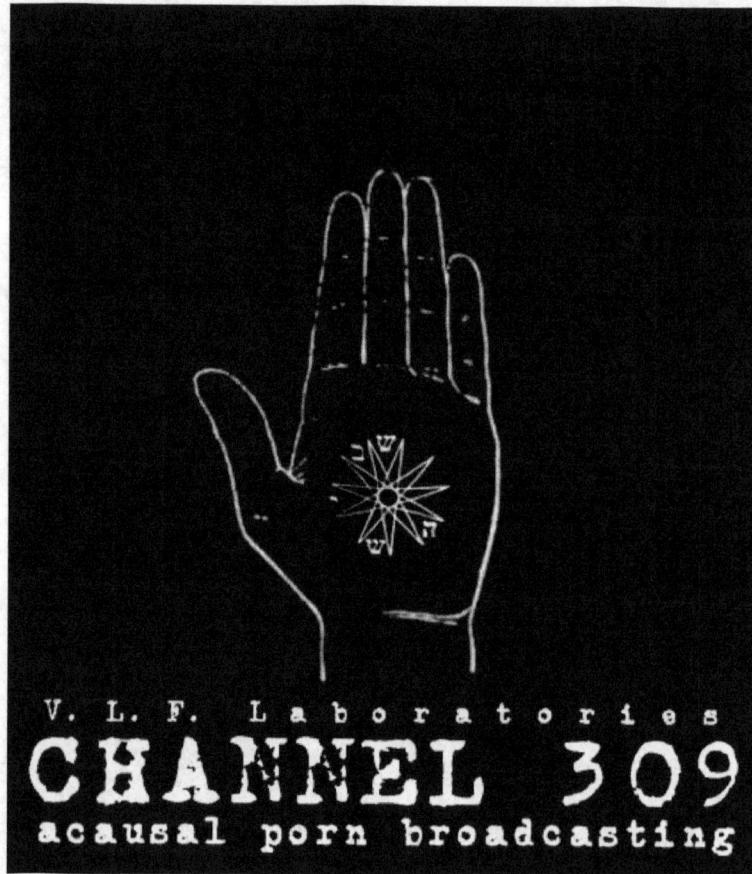

V.L.F. Laboratories
CHANNEL 309
acausal porn broadcasting

www.vlfvideo.blogspot.com

07

VERBUM I – A STATEMENT FROM THE ORDER OF MIZBACH.

JOHN HOPE

I was asked if I would offer a brief and preliminary summary of the recently incepted Thelemic Vamachara British LHP order currently known as the O.M. or the Order of Mizbach, a dynamically organised, encapsidated Outer formation for a long, pre-existing hereditary lineage originating from Dorset. The cell itself is now currently based in the New Forest and Bournemouth areas of Dorset and operates jointly between Ireland and the South West counties of England.

I will do my best here to describe our fundamental philosophy, without going too much into the ritual praxes of the group. With the Law of Thelema we cultivate a combined practice of spiritually transmitted ritual, and hereditary lore.

The Arkay Agam Mageia comes from the Hebrew for the *First Lake of Magic*. This is used to describe in a way our psychical and ancient lineage.

The lineage has now been consolidated and set firm as our current LHP Order. We have expressed in previous notes that the group is a physically and spiritually active and dynamic one in its nature. We strongly oppose the lazy occultist, or fair-weather magician.

To express and generate our fraternal inculcation we are heavily eclectic and utilise (often very obscure) praxis from many different cultures and ancient systems, in most cases these are all branching from the same source of occult truth and magick. It may be best to analyse and look into folk lore and customs from the oldest sources possible, that way we have less pollution and a better fix on the truthful gnosis of each magickal system, less tainted by modern re-interpretations.

The Order independently follows the 93 Current in all of its creative dynamism and does not attempt to influence fellow member with anything to do with the personal perceptions of what Thelema means to the individual. By their very nature some Outer Orders or groups follow in an almost orthodox fashion what has gone before, and never stray far from the tracks. This is one of the principle reasons why we use the Greek term *Katharosian* (purged, clean or pure) to describe the particular means and nature of our approach to Thelemic practise. Real Magic(k) and Thelema in our opinion are dynamic and forever changing modes of our

Sabbatic-gnostic practice. Our familial-hereditary and spiritual authority involves the ultra-cultural memes of true Traditional Witchcraft. The Kashaph, or Kohen Jadu are our initiated witches, the first degree of only two graded states of being within the Cell, and they operate on their own magickal terms and intuition.

The Order does not involve itself with the giving of its member's doctrines, interpretations or group ritual. Each initiate follows his or her own Thelemic path and personally divined ritual practice. One of the major differences between us and the various other Thelemic groups in operation is that membership is only activated by a spiritual entity over a designated period of 49 days. The profound nature of his membership process naturally serves as an occult filter. Through the very nature of the self are we given a method to separate the magickal wheat from the chaff. This should not be seen as elitism, on the contrary... The aspirant is self-initiated during the 49 day probation, and then if they are ready, there will occur an explicit, direct manifestation. During this episode the individual will be sealed within the circle of the Mizbe'ah as a consecration of their I°. The entire process is obviously not to be taken lightly. As we work with real spiritual entities dangers will present themselves if the correct protective pre-cautions are not taken, and remember that a spiritual

poisoning from one foolhardy contact can result in lasting damages both spiritually and mentally.

As a group we recognize the importance of utilizing the Fourth Power of the Sphinx (Hoor-paar-Kraat), and we have a peculiar practice called Spekan Silentium (the sacred dumah), or the art of Speaking in Silence, the application and subsequent realisation of which leads us to (amongst other things) the cultivation of powerful creative psychic energies.

This is a key step to the inner katharos of the O.M. and involves the contemplation of the Word's binary power of manifestation (similarly we have 2 hands, 2 eyes, etc.). We may see this through Chokhmah and the 7 – 1 antecedent aspect in Ajna.

We welcome members from all magickal & spiritual paths. Initiation into the O.M. can of course occur when the individual is already a member of another order; dual membership does in no way affect the process of personal activation within this Cell. This process of the giving of spiritual authority, or 'activation' mentioned earlier is what is known as the Unum Adapertiol, or the rite of the ONE OPENING, and is in itself the binding inner Cingulum and outer grounding of our members. To clarify further, the Order occupies itself with an independently transmitted modus of

(Traditional) witchcraft, symbiotically nurtured with the Law of Thelema. This is the real *Virtus of the Mageia*. Those with a genuine interest in the activity of our group are here welcomed to contact the Magister for more information by emailing the editor, who will provide relevant contact details.

THE ART OF
EDGAR KERVAL

APEP

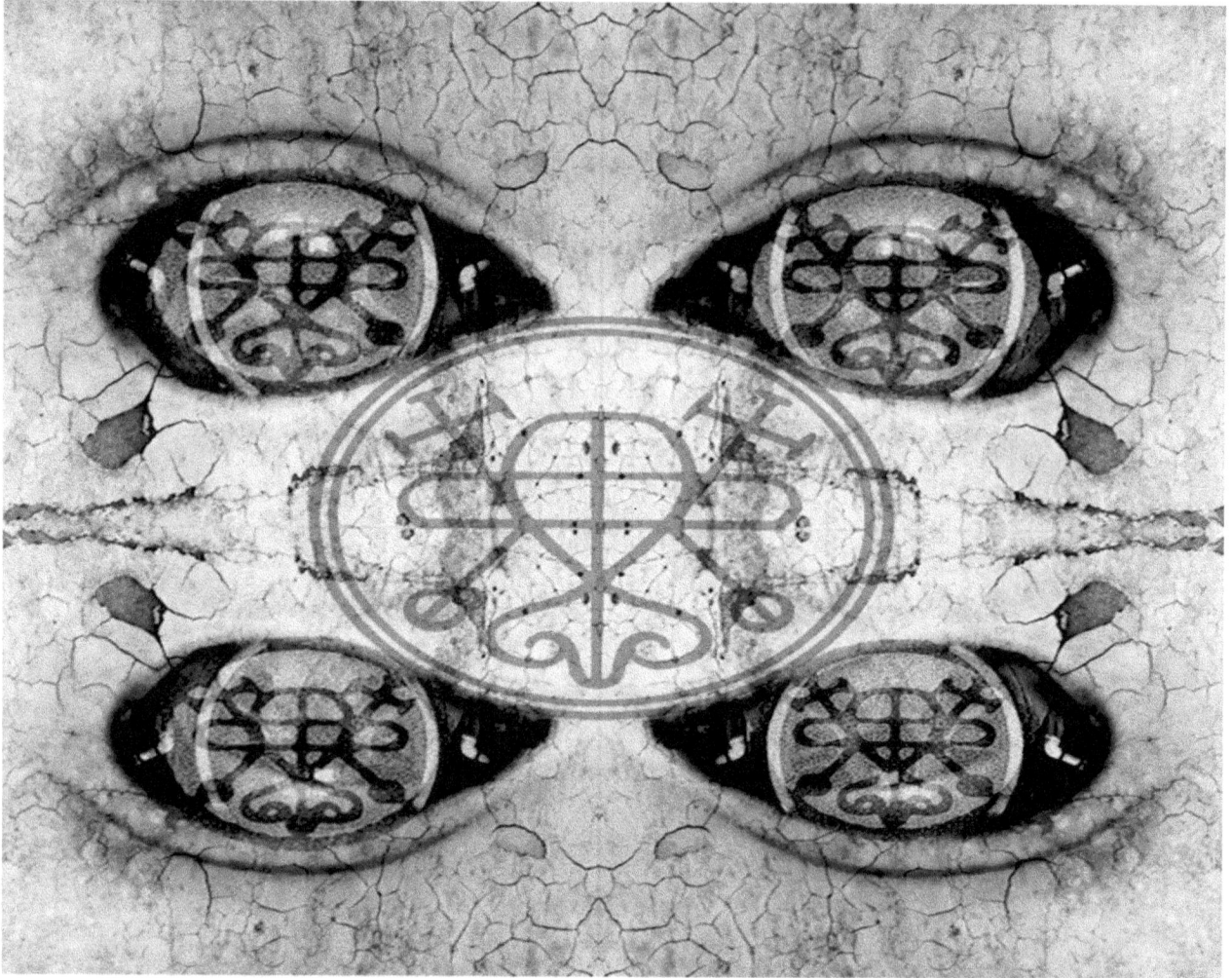

BAEL

GUARDIAN OV THE SEVENTH TEMPLE

LERA'S TORMENT

Aubrey Wood Basnight

PROLOGUE

Amme stood before him sheathed from head to toe in a vinyl suit of sable hue - the sadistic black glistening amidst the low-glowing orbs surrounding the fell cavernous chamber and accentuated by the strikes of lightning from beyond the gaping windows allowing passage for the nocturnal darkness inside the walls of the keep. No panes nor grills covered the opening and only a foot-deep indention into the masonry stone separated the inside of the tower from the yawning several-thousand foot drop onto the treacherous precipice, which served as the stony boundary for the lands below and beneath.

Never did he consider that his self-inflicted torment would lead him into this situation - only in the most vivid fantasies and unrequited nightmares. For years he had contemplated the merciless visage of that goddess - collecting in every form and medium those forms and mediums, which showed her likeness, indicating to him her hideous quintessence. Sometimes unforgiving in countenance, often shrewd - sometimes merciless, rarely benign. It did not matter in the slightest, for her every variation of poise and gesture pierced like hot needles into his very soul. And now, at long last, Max's soul was hers for the taking.

It was the small man in the desert town who had shown him the way to consummate those deepest desires. Smiling as he was on the journey, a business trip he had said, in a manner of speaking, to a North American clime where they first met. He told in great detail of the objects of power which he possessed - a certain object in particular, which would be a needful thing for the proclivities of the intrepid seeker. He changed his mind often as to whether he possessed them or whether he knew the person, or knew the person who knew the person, who might provide Max with what he sought for no small sum. Money however was not the object - so he soothed in his descriptions. For the diadems which he possessed for those seeking the ultimate in cruelty and passion themselves found those who were appropriate - those special, those selected, the desert dweller had stated authoritatively. He and by guilty association those others whom he sometimes intimated were only the vectors by which the appropriate assignations could be arranged between bearer and beholder, between traveler and gate-keeper. Such selfless souls, ha! If this was a pact with the devil, then the dealer was the solicitor only, there as witness for the signatories. Even then, Max did not buy into the transactional soft padding which was put forward in search of a buyer. But, in reality, the prospective buyers for such items of no small rarity had little care, the elaborate sales-pitch being unnecessary (a fact which the seller probably knew) – for the object of lust far transcended any dithering over what was really, in the larger scheme of things, small and insignificant particulars.

It was with those thoughts in mind that Max made the transatlantic flight – flying coach and in the most austere class, and contracting with the most Third World airline he could manage to find servicing outbound flights, for the more ample contents of his purse would be needed for the more important transaction to come (he could suffer much in the interim – though he would suffer greater, as it were, in the end). Jet-lagged and physicality in abject despair, yet mind and consciousness alight with the glowing thought – that unshakeable feeling of what was to come – he made his way from the airport to the dingy, squalid room in which he was to spend the night. Cash flowing somewhat more freely now, in premeditation of the final destination, the usual bribes of the taxi attendants were met with no argument, much to their delight – his mind somewhat amiss to his surroundings, albeit widely exotic. For far

more exotic treats lay in store for Max, as he contemplated to himself, not in the sweet by and by, but as soon as the next day's mid-morning scheduled meeting.

The next day was met with a frightful dawning. Every muscle and every fiber of his brain said to sleep, sleep, sleep! Rest the self that needs its rest, repine upon the nasty yet soft (softer indeed than the torture-racks that passed for seating in the C-class airline upon which he had spent ten continual hours the day/night before, the time-change being somewhat of a blur and a nuisance to consider) spring-loaded mattress. So what if the meeting was missed? Risk nothing, lose nothing. He was frugal by design and by circumstance but hardly impoverished – he could eat the expense, as the saying goes. Take in the local flora and fauna, perhaps upgrade to more hospitable digs in the process for a few days, no less (as his return ticket was ticked for departure only a few days from now). Make it a small vacation. His miniscule number of associates would understand – though that would hardly matter, all things being equal. He was many years isolated – a lone-wolf bred in the bone. Should he expire in the midst of this voyage, how long would it be before any connected to him – even in the most titular sense – would realize it? He shifted the thought from his mind, as he went about his business in preparation for the morning meeting.

Ah, and there it came. Although thinking himself, convincing himself of some degree of indifference to the event which loomed before him - which he had thought to eschew, casually, no less, he had - as if flying on auto-pilot (the aeronautics connotations perhaps another lingering malady of his slowly - ever-so-slowly lessening jet-lag) put himself square and center about preparations for just that purpose and at a soldier's pace. Somewhat smelly clothing shed, a few minutes under the indisputably insufficient dribble of what passed for a showerhead - though water, thankfully hot - more than like courtesy of the regional climate than the performance of the establishment's hot-water heater, if it was within a fraction of the disrepair of the rest of the joint. Then, there - fresh clothing donned, passport stowed safely in back pocket of corduroy trousers, leather shoulder satchel hoisted and hooked on shoulder of due preference and sturdy collegiate backpack held by the upper hook, he was ready. Sunglasses steamed with his own breath - wiped clean, or cleaner at least, with edge of chambray shirt soon tucked into waistband. Checking about for keys in hand to room for latter re-entry - preferably with the item for which this long journey had been the very point. Good, noted, affirmative - with a few swift steps and the soft thud of the door, he was off.

THE DESERT
Part 1

Beyond the confines of his night quarters, the thrum and cacophony of the eastern city brayed with a mania and violence unknown to those who kept within the safe, subdued boundaries of North America, Europe, and Scandinavia. The harsh glare of the desert sun put every crevice of the metropolis into bold, blasphemous, stark naked relief. The layers upon layers of filth built up over decades upon the walls of the buildings, their white paint flecking, revealing the primitive crudity of the masonry beneath. The smudged soot upon the faces of the small gang of child labourers, metal buckets containing oily tools in hand, who walked in single file up the gangplank upon a market roof and then descended through a cloud of foul-smelling smoke of unknown origin on the other side. A swarm of flies buzzed angrily around a large and bloody pile of severed ram's heads, the thick juices of their decapitation flowing lazily into the gutter. Another dozen or so down, he mused, in the questionable cause of the Black Sultan. And all of this, mind, amidst the ringing of hammer upon steely anvils, livestock, bleating horns in natural stereophonics with bleating goats, peeling rubber. He licked his dry lips, turning left off the main thoroughfare.

He was in the slums and no doubt about it. But what sort of area did he expect as a meeting place for obtaining the sort of object – or perhaps that very singular, none other like it, black market of black market good to dim all other variation of illegal transaction imaginable – which bore the blackest of reputations? Most others would already be well out of their depth and none too put off simply by the country where the meeting had been decided – put forward by the dealers that is, little input on that from the prospective purchaser. After all, they had all the cards. All of the deck and so much more. That being the case, he himself was not too off put by the location – being a world-traveler by dint of habit and in those long solitary years having seen similar regions, some of them worse, in fact. But there was no arguing that the specific area in which they had chosen for the liaison was particularly grotesque, even by his cosmopolitan standards.

No mind, eyes on the prize. Even though many eyes were upon him – though only a trained eye would notice. The thieves, young and old, slinking here and there in the alleyways between the butcher's and the tailor's shop-slash-opium den, the draconian police of the reigning monarch, the black tools of repression hanging with dread upon black leather belts cinched about broad bodies which oozed brutality. And then the myriad security and intelligence agents – those domestic and those from abroad who tended to gather like a murder in the region and for whom the sight of a foreign national well off the beaten tourist and official business trails would attract their very keen attention.

These latter he left mostly unnoticed, let them watch he thought, though he was aware of their presence nonetheless. There would be time enough for evasion on the flight back, after he had acquired the needful. Flight-times could be changed (or cancelled). He could live quite conscionably with a small sabbatical for concentration, in country, as his scheduled work after this ordeal was over, pending acquisition, did not necessarily depend on any specific geographic location per se. Barring immediate flight abroad, back to his usual country of residence from the nearby international airport and up and away from the city in which he now found himself he could opt for a train across the border and then flight homeward. Or even more elaborate, perhaps a winding and uncomfortable, but not necessarily (not necessarily, he reminded himself) contracted van or private vehicle across the tribal areas – across the desert and seldom watched borders – into another country, then another and then, there, perhaps, some time alone – for experimentation. And then, then perhaps, an eventual return to the sprawling house which he inhabited infrequently, by right, trusting, knowing, that it would still be uninhabited. Yet there were as the case may be any number of potential variables. That he knew for certain – that brooding and incessant uncertainty of his life and especially, vehemently felt, the uncertainty of his present venture.

The situation on the street once he had made his final turn was no less hectic than the main road, though it was narrow enough that only the most impetuous of drivers would attempt it. No less hectic, despite the relative absence of vehicular traffic, yet perhaps moreso in fact in that the teeming life of the slum had been compacted by some absence of ten feet or so width compared to the larger streets and thus all the more crowded by foot traffic, hoof traffic and sundry. Bouncing off the decaying mortar and stucco walls the screams of the infants, the wailing of the women, the basso curses of the men, whether in ferocious earnest or the showy bombast of the trained and seasoned haggler, all seemed to conspire to cave in on the collective temporary residents – human, animal and non-sentient alike.

As he proceeded down the drive – little more than a largish alley in reality, albeit long (there was no foreseeable end in sight, courtesy of the rabble and other rather distasteful environmental factors) he noticed a peculiar phenomena in comparison to his early peregrinations thus far in departing

his morbid temporary flat. From the corner of his eyes and periphery vision it seemed to him that the alley was slowly closing in on itself from behind. Not wanting to turn around outright, as to avoid too suspicious of behavior in lieu of the overt and covert security he recognized before, what to speak of the potential intelligence, he could not shake the revelation of what began to be a clear theme since he had made that fateful sharp turn left.

The market people, vagrants and beggars, crowded as before, without question, but still keeping to the sides of the road then, at least somewhat – allowing passage this way and that – had begun to coalesce behind him up to the intersection in the center of the road, easing themselves into a wider fray, essentially blocking any further traffic after he had entered.

Several fights broke out, verbal but by the sheer sound level of said verbiage promising perhaps more rapturous manifestation in the by and by, between irate stall-keeper and irate customer; between upright feminine coolie and cocky single-digit beggars of the boyish persuasion.

A few uniformed police from the mainstreet edged in on the action as it occurred, beefy hands upraised and spittle-laced bellows issuing forth loudly at no disturber of the peace in particular, yet attached beefy arms seemed to also be blocking certain persons from the scene - namely the florid-faced and obviously western man in safari clothes too new and pristine, too contrived, beedy eyes scanning the crowd to and fro in want of a certain someone whose location had now, suddenly, escaped his grasp. Likewise for the olive-skinned, beak-nosed bespectacled someone or other, more aggressive and assertive than his Anglo counterpart, who tried to duck under the throng of the spectator adults only to find his way irrevocably blocked by dozens of shouting youth who seemed to coalesce - as if on cue - beneath his feet - battling for a bit of copper that in all likelihood did not exist except in their own contrivance.

The closure was orchestrated, without a doubt, but the question in his mind was by whom? Was a security professional - domestic and/or private and/or contracted on the ample dole of the crown - waiting for him up ahead, the scenario arranged precisely and well-padded with universal currency so that they could have choice pickings for the interdiction of a foreign interloper dead-set on the acquisition of what was perhaps an artifact banned for transport out of the host country? Or was it the dread portents of fate - working in his favor - or even disfavor depending on perspective - clearing the board, stacking the deck, so that he could make his way,

unencumbered, to his previously scheduled assignation?

His thoughts were interrupted as he passed straight through the first intersection since his turn - the crossing street not nearly as narrow as his own forward route but still amply populated with through traffic. He felt his bowels clench and loosen simultaneously. If he was to be extraordinarily renditioned, this would be the place.

His ponderings were broken again - perhaps accentuated - by multiple brutal shoves upon his back. The people behind him had made their pace more brisk even as his own became more sluggish in lieu of circumspection and he found himself being pushed involuntarily across the intersection and on into the even more close-quartered avenue, the clanging of the various metals and screeching of the surrounding mob becoming even more disturbing.

The demographics on this block were deucedly darker than those he had encountered earlier and it appeared that the mob scene had done its trick - no visible surveillance had followed him - at least insofar as he could ascertain, still being pushed incessantly along by the throng behind him.

All at once the mad rush stopped as a roaring truck engine announced itself along with several long blasts upon its formidable horn, the sound of which was immediately followed by the ululating of all the women present whom, like their male counterparts, had stopped dead in their tracks – excepting those still in the intersection proper, who jumped aside avoiding the path of the oncoming truck.

Max did not see the cause for the commotion immediately, his eyes instead lingering in the opposite direction on two elderly blind women, clad in conservative black, who hunkered down on the ground beside one of the walls of one the of many derelict buildings in the area, eagerly whispering to each other betwixt raising their own heads and ululating themselves with toothless, grinning mouths, their eyes concealed under the shade of their cowls. One of the women pointed her long, bony finger emphatically toward the intersection and he decided to take the cue to proffer greeting to the oncoming commotion at very least by viewing, though sans the verbal greeting issuing forth from the mouths of the two elderly ladies toward whatever procession was beginning to pass, doubting his ability to do so and noting, with a sense of propriety and reserve that all of the other men in the street remained silent.

Turning somewhat abruptly and nearly tripping over a haggard tomcat who raised his hackles in offended protest, hissing profoundly at him before scurrying off, he found his footing at last and stared along with the rest of his human compatriots on what proved to be a most grisly spectacle indeed – though the initial gore horror was to be mixed with a latter dread beauty, though possessing even in cursory inspection a potentially even more horrific intent within – and thus, a harbinger of things to come.

PART 2

This type of thing had been witnessed by him before, though this was without a doubt more devastating in visual effect in several distinct ways than what he had seen prior according to his mental travelogue for comparison. The closest similar event most readily comparable would be the Thaipusam he witnessed in his early twenties at the base of the steep stairway to the Batu Caves – having travelled to Malaysia for that specific event and destination.

He had known little about the purpose of the ritual itself at the time, other than the fact that it had an elaborate and legendary obscene pageantry involving profuse mortification of the flesh and self-mutilation in fashions only known and practiced by the most underground elements in the west (and those still, falling well short). That and the proliferation of the unique spiritism-laced drumming present only in the former territories of the Chola empire, engineered specifically to induce trance and possession, audial examples of which a friend at the university had recorded and brought back on a reel-to-reel which he had borrowed repeatedly during his freshman year.

The event in progress at the intersection was much different however – as was his perception of the same comparatively – his rather devil-may-care attitude of more youthful years seeming like an increasingly ancient memory in differentiation to the paranoia that began in his early thirties and had continued apace since that time.

He remembered when he had arrived in Malaysia and made his way to the market area, which catered to the celebrants some days before the Thaipusam festival those many years ago, inquiring – despite his not knowing Murugan that much from Mohammad in all honesty – about participating in the festivities himself. The young Tamilan running the stand selling cold coconut milk smiled broadly before laughing, good naturedly, as he surveyed the eager westerner who stood before him with a Kool cigarette in one hand and a large bottle of Guinness in the other, before explaining to him that a mandatory period

of purification was required in order to bear *kavadi.*

All this had been taken by Max in stride, though he did later wonder whether or not the chemical and sexual ban indicated by his informant had been entirely correct or whether he had simply been engaging in dialogue with a more conservative observer when he saw almost identical large bottles of Guinness (and lager, and toddy) being consumed by the shirtless men with bulging red-rimmed bloodshot eyes during the ceremony proper who busied themselves with taking enormous draws from big stinking cigars and gracious hits of the aforementioned myriad alcoholic beverages betwixt flagellating themselves with thick hauling chains.

This particular demographic however was only one sector of the procession – the much larger being (and a reluctant nod to his informant here) those who seemed stoic – near blank – as attendant brahmins busied themselves rubbing scores of proffered backs with sacred ash before inserting fish-hooks with surgical precision into the pale spots on dark flesh, some of which bore speared limes attached to small weights and others brass pots containing various offerings. Then there were those with the sharpened metal rods, ornate ends attached either side after penetration, the vel within the vetri vel chant resounding across the immensely populated base to the mountain, piercing their cheeks and then others with similar ceremonial spears inserted through the tongue - some smallish, some medium in size and others so gargantuan that the relative proportions to their bearers defied all logic.

The main and most notable difference between that experience and the one he now witnessed was blood - that being most specifically the absence of or surplus quantities thereof. For reasons which he had studied only well after the fact, the participants in Thaipusam apparently shed no blood whatsoever in pursuit of their disciplines - no matter how deep the piercing, no matter how arduous the burden (or as a more proper reference of the mechanism borne by some, *kavadi*).

Some physical scientists had proffered reasons for this peculiar phenomena, mystics and devotees still another. But the fact remained. For all the mutilatory excess that typified a south Indian-style propitiation of the gods and goddesses of war, the spillage of human life-force in its well-recognized and trademark reddish incarnation was not only muted but entirely nonexistent in those proceedings. Not so, not now, in this remote slum amidst an increasingly nightmarish desert outpost.

No music marred the ceremonial procession, no shouts of encouragement came from the crowd, though the audial presence was still significant. While physically still, the watchers after a few minutes of pause resumed engagement in multiple conversations. Whether or not the exchanges were related to what they were witnessing was beyond him, his Arabic being only elementary, though the talks lacked the notable shrillness that he had witnessed before. The sounds of commerce, animal husbandry, animal butchery and other sundry activities of the ghetto still continued apace, amidst the white noise sounds of traffic from afar and the distinct rumbling of the truck as its made its way up the corridor - announcing via the auspices of compressed air its sounds of warning for the few yet unaware crossing pedestrians and revving its engine in complementary fashion. That being said there was still a certain distinguishable stillness - as if his own perception of hearing perhaps and perhaps that of the other spectators as well in kind was lessened, so that the eyes predominant and alone could take in the incomparable ghastliness of the scene.

Streams of blood issued forth from increasingly severe wounds which opened themselves upon the backs and shaven heads of the members of the procession. Amongst the former, ragged chains holding a fan of small chains, each with small blackened blades, though revealing recently attended to and razor-sharp edges moved forward and back and forward and back again in rigid whipping fashion, the intimidating implements repeating the process with grim continuity as increasing rivulets of the crimson life blood of the faithful poured down upon bare backs, staining the waistbands of the simple white trousers cinched against thin and fat bellies alike.

For the latter, similarly crude but cruelly edged knives were held aloft proudly, some with curved blades and others ramrod straight in their machining, grasped in their dominant hand as the bearers muttered to themselves indistinguishably, whether oaths or prayers he could not tell, before gouging their heads again and again in brutal fashion and with fanatic intent, causing blood and clots to sometimes ooze, sometimes pour, cascading down upon their faces held in rapt-attention, congealing in black beards both great and small.

The women ululated, the men (those not participating, that is) stared with no great interest but with well rehearsed reverence, having seen this sort of thing many times before no doubt, as the smell of fresh blood beginning and salty sweat began to predominate in the stale dry air, mixing in with the odors of compact bodies, animal feces, smelting iron and curing leather.

Max, as his passport indicated (a name which he had used increasingly since his late teens, though not his given name at birth) also stared - attention much more rapt than his other observing counterparts - growing even more   attentive as the parade continued, the distinct verbal salutations of the ladies present becoming much more pronounced as the object of zenith began snaking its way toward his line of vision.

PART 3

The line of participants began to thin as the sight of a large litter began to crawl into their line of vision - stout cedar beams carried by well-muscled bearded men, these unmarred and unbloodied, their own strength reserved for a particular purpose which made the excesses of their fellows ahead of them impractical.

Atop the beams were large cedar planks, twenty foot long and at least an inch thick, the cost of which would be too dear to imagine in the Americas. These supported large, several inch-thicker mattress-like constructions arranged together to create an impression of seamlessness, gilded in the finest embroided golden filigree and bordered with rounded pillows equally embellished by the artisanal work of a seasoned and skilled upholsterer.

Upon all this, on a cushioned throne similarly adorned, sat a girl of eleven or twelve, as regal as any queen enhanced by the timbre of her entourage at least as deadly, if not more so.

Though adorned in the shimmering rich fabrics of the region, some draped about her head in an attempt to be demure as local custom dictated, Max saw clearly that the striking brown eyes that surveyed the crowd were of lightish brown hazel, bespeaking the manicured and maintained Elizabethan manor houses of southern England rather than the crumbling medieval ruins of a North African fortress. Pale skin, a haughty bearing of a secular rather than religious bent and long curls of brown hair rupturing about the neckline of her loose garments only confirmed his suspicions.

Was she the real reason behind the orchestrated block of the (his assumption) British or American intelligent agent and the other foreign national - likely Israeli (what to speak of those who had not registered on his radar) - from entering the sideway, rather than he? Some British cult goddess - perhaps kidnapped - perhaps the child Manchurian candidate of some eldritch foreign power flying under false front but obviously, as the procession would indicate, wielding serious influence on her own behalf and on behalf of those of her control?

He stood in rapture - heedless to the pushing and shoving about him of the hometown residents beginning to rouse at last from their rather perfunctory observation and commencing to go about their business once again in earnest - treading forward this way and that in the opposite directions, on through and beginning to crowd the absent areas of the intersection, pushing themselves into the adjoining street and on toward the back of the procession, making their way around the dwindling blockage.

Behind the litter there were a few persons only who seemed to be official participants - these neither carrying splayed knife-bearing chain whips nor holding aloft similar knives designed for a similar blood-letting purpose. Rather only a handful of men, markedly more muscular and intimidating than their counterparts - though the intimidation factor of persons who consisted of the vanguard of the march, those dripping in their own blood which had been spilled by their own will and design could not easily be denied - if they could do that to themselves, what would they be willing to do to others? The stature of these persons inhabiting the back portion of the procession were instead bearing an aura of threat in an implicit rather than explicit fashion - though the threat was certainly there. While not of a dint that would indicate professional intelligence, the circumstances here being perhaps too open and overt for that particular type, he could certainly believe that these men, whatever their trade in the normative day-to-day sense, could at least be moonlighting as force protection (as they were doing now, in a sense) or acting within professional security capacities. A few off-duty (or even plaint clothed) police-officers in the mix would not be beyond reason. The telltale signs of handheld firearms could be intimated from bulges around their middles and beneath jackets casual in appearance yet tactical in design.

His eyes set only ever so briefly upon this demographic however, his more immediate concern being holding himself upright – in the center of the thoroughfare – no less, amidst the pushings and proddings of hundreds passing this way and that – and keeping his eyes squarely on the female who rode in the style of royalty on the litter which was passing by all too quickly – for less than a minute remained before the vision of her would be lost to him, crossing the visual threshold beyond the walls of the decrepit building to the left which served as the corner of the city block. He attempted to press forward – reversing his course – back in the direction from which he had come – further toward the intersection – but foreign shouted curses and painful elbows aimed toward his person, voluntarily or involuntary in the course of the flow of traffic and its ebb and tide – made it all he could muster to stand his ground with

forced rigidity and watch as the image of the fell empress passed slowly before him.

He stared intensely – fanatically even – hoping that somehow, by some potency unbeknownst to his person and defying all natural laws as laid down by mundane researchers of natural sciences – that he could draw her attention, if only for a moment. Doubting this dubious ability but not bending to the increasing temptation to make a spectacle of himself – waving his arms – yelling – screaming – such acts which would perhaps be misconstrued by the object of his devotion (should she deign to notice) or the security personnel which followed her to the rear (which would likely result in violence done upon his person – preventative from their perspective for what might be perceived as either a dangerous, provocative or simply a potentially disruptive reaction of the over-enthusiastic) he opted to simply raise both arms and hands outstretched – aloft as high as he could muster – Caitanya-like in effect and intent – keeping his position unmoving and his gaze steady.

In a moment which seemed like the passing of ages, though which was in all reality only a few seconds since he had affected his gesture (though the affectation was more genuine than not) he saw her turn her head – slowly, ever so slowly – the pacing and timbre of the gesture unmistakably bespeaking aristocracy bred into blood and bone in its practiced physical elocution – and, for a few brief seconds, he saw her gaze rest upon him, imperious. The lines around her vivid brown eyes crinkled ever so slightly, her brow knotting quizzically in a gesture as unrehearsed and primordially breathtaking as a simultaneously vast but divinely anomalous manifest stand of ancient primeval forest – before she threw back her head, revealing ever so precious pale neckline, the covering of her hair nearly falling down onto her upper back as she laughed lustfully.

As soon as it had occurred – that singular moment of delight and recognition – she tilted her head forward once again, the briefest hint of a lingering smile upon her soft reddish lips, natural and not tainted by the sort of garish makeup that would paint the lips of a similarly situated kumari in state. One last look toward him again from her – eye to eye across the populated mass and then her head turned forward – toward the direction of her acolytes marching before her in grim, blood-covered state, toward the now distant truck which continued to announce her coming via alternating blast of airhorn and unnecessary but dramatic and attention-seeking gear-grinding snarl of gasoline-driven accelerator recognition. Then – just so, almost as if it had never happened at all – she was gone – a last sight of her presence being the sight of the end strands of her silken garment blowing behind her, caught up in the currents of the foul wind. Arms still outstretched to the polluted heavens, tears, unbidden, began to flow down his cheeks in awe, reverence and the instantaneously occurring pangs of separation.

THE ART OF
NESTOR AVALOS

THE LOUISIANA CULLING

LEOPOLD LAWRENCE

PREPARATIONS

What I plan on doing is of no consequence. It is only what I will do that will speak for itself. For I plan on committing that which cannot be committed, the Perfect Crime. No, I'm no Raskolnikov. I have no intention of murdering an old lady just so I get a feel of what it feels to have the blood of others on my hands. The death of one insignificant soul is, like me, of no consequence. For I seek casualties in the hundreds if not thousands!

Indeed, for me to commit what I now seek to do, I have had to meditate and consult the Sinister Forces for months on end. Like the things beyond this world, the Sinister forces do not always readily answer to human needs, nor would they have to since they exist beyond in the Acausal Realm which humans have only marginal access to it if they have not travelled beyond them through Astral Travel.

I will not bother you with the details of this ritual since such things are beyond the comprehension of mere Mundanes who only live along the Causal realm of physics and materiality. However, in the past months of consulting the Sinister forces, I've seen them manifest regularly on a day-to-day basis, egging me on to do that which I've sought to do. Often these manifestations are all too subtle for the naked human eye but they can also manifest in more spectacular ways. The more visible signs are all there: mass shootings, acts of terror, and mass violence abound as things are veering towards total collapse. I welcome all of this as an active agent of Chaos!

The fact is, this World is in need of a massive culling on a global scale and it must start from individual acts of terror and chaos, an act of the 'propaganda of the deed' that will serve as a call to action to other agents of Chaos against the forces of tyrannical Order, against the State, against a decadent civilization that can no longer stand on its own two feet. It is a world of lame cripples and spiritual crassness where those who espouse 'religion' give their followers tokens of false hope that serves only as a delusion for these utterly hopeless and despairing folk. So they consult the frauds, the priests, in the hopes that they can save them from their own self-damnation. These frauds sooth these idiots by giving them a sense of false hope and meaning in a world that lacks both of these things and these willing slaves become addicted to this! After all, false hope and meaning is a potent drug to numb one to all of life's miseries.

Because they're too weak to find it in themselves, the Mundanes find their meaning in their own submission to abstractions and to temporal masters who promise them happiness and wealth if they only work a bit harder and consumer a bit more. To be happy consumers and producers! They admire those who tell them how great they are, or how great they could potentially be, those who shower them with unbelievable promises of a better life on 'faith' alone. So they obey willingly, the happy slaves they all are! These people are surely contemptible but enough of them! I'm too repulsed by them to even talk of them anymore for a life has only 'meaning' once it has acted on its mission that it has set for itself. And my own life has set me upon this path of pure destruction that I am now on. And words only have meaning when they are no longer words but conjurings of greater deeds to come!

NEW ORLEANS

It is Mardi-Gras in New Orleans. The many people have rushed onto the streets of the French Quarter along Bourbon Street as they indulge in a night of pure drunkenness and other assorted frivolities. This will continue for another week and allow me the time to plan and orchestrate my plans to perfection.

I walked across Bourbon St. on a noisy Thursday night, as I minded the crowd which gathered every which way by the thousands as drunkards and mundanes of all kinds made a scene of themselves; from party-goers to old men looking to get laid one last time to women baring their breasts to passer-bys for some beads.

So I moved amongst and against the crowd not giving a damn about any of this. A handful of police officers lined the streets, covering the many corners and alleyways of the streets of the French Quarter. You could see a few of them in their blue-black uniforms and their bright-yellow raincoats questioning passer-bys, many of them drunk. One of these cops was actively harassing a homeless man on the streets. Some were on horses conducting their night patrols, batons to the side and walkie-talkies at the ready. These cops would need to be carefully noticed if my plans were to go in accordance with my own Sinister Will. After all, the forces of Order have their own plans that were in direct opposition to mine.

But the night was getting rainy, as some of the mundanes made their way indoors into the many clubs and hotels that lined Bourbon Street and beyond. There was a brightly lit promenade decorated with lanterns and roses that made its way towards a certain Spanish Colonial-era building (the French Quarter was populated with such kinds of buildings) which functioned as a bar and hotel. The hotel's name was "the Mississippi Riverboat". I planned on meeting Seamus there inside their bar tomorrow. He had promised to supply me with the arms and explosives to carry out this great massacre. Moreover, his active participation would also be necessary to implement it. This would the most important thing of our meeting and I required his full support. But first I had to check-in.

A young woman greeted me with a hearty smile at the entrance as I made my way into the hotel. She welcomed me to their hotel, trying to make small-talk with me.

"Hello sir, welcome to the Mississippi Riverboat!"

I gave her a weak smile and replied, "I've got a reservation for a room at your hotel. Can you show me the way to the reception?"

"Right this way sir, it's near the back," she told me with the most irritating smile that I could fathom.

"Thank you."

Sure enough, she pointed her arm towards the reception at the back as she moved her attention towards an old couple, probably retired, who were behind me and had just made their way into the hotel with their luggage in tow. By the reception, a balding middle-aged Black man took my bank card and ID as he confirmed my reservation on his computer. You could hear him coughing as he was busily typing away.

"Well, I've got you a room at the 4th floor, room 450. Would that be alright with you?" he inquired.

"No problem that will do for me."

He gave me back my card and ID. Then he took the suitcase that I had with me and motioned to a young but thick-set valet beside him. He gave him my suitcase with instructions to carry it up to my room telling the valet, "show our kind client to his room. That's his suitcase, don't wreck it."

I was somewhat reluctant to release my suit to this valet. But he took it anyways.

"Right this way, sir" said the valet as he guided me towards the escalator.

I was dreading this annoying hospitality on the part of the hotel staff. All I wanted was to meet Seamus as soon as possible and get his active cooperation for my project, that is, *our project.*

At the escalator, the valet was busying himself away whistling a tune and shuffling his feet along the carpeted floor of the escalator with my suitcase in hand. I glanced him a look and then turned my head to the side. We reached the 4th floor and got out. I didn't trust him with my suitcase.

The only person on the floor was the cleaning lady who was vacuuming the carpet. She seemed fatigued and bored out of her mind as she mumbled some words to herself in what sounded like Spanish. I guessed she was Puerto Rican. The valet finally showed me to my room as we crisscrossed the floor, making twists and turns until we got to room 450 which was by a corner and a fire exit, convenient for making an easy escape just in case anything goes wrong.

"Here's your room sir and thanks for staying with us," he said, perhaps routinely, as he handed me back my suitcase. I took it from him and quickly got into the room, closing the door shut behind me.

I gently placed my suitcase on top of the bed, it was a thick Queen-size bed whose clean white sheets smelled as if they had just been recently replaced. Then, I took a quick wash in the bathroom, shaved my face and looked at myself in the mirror. I could have looked a lot worse, the flight from Chicago took longer than I thought and I hadn't slept in the past day. My eyes were beginning to show my fatigue.

Without regarding this, however, I went back to grab my suitcase which I flipped open and took out some photos showing the different targets and places of interest that would be filled with tourists at this time of the year. I laid these photos on the bed too. There was also a ritual candle, two of them, and some cigars that my girlfriend had prepared for me. In there, I had also packed my old, sheathed battle knife; a WWI-era German bayonet which had been passed down to me by my great-grandfather to my grandfather then to my father and then to me. The edge along the handle was a bit rusty and worse-for-wear but it was a durable and reliable knife which I trusted with my life.

In my suitcase was also the text, 'the Magister Book', which I had consulted for presenting the Sinister forces. The book itself was dated to the mid-16th century and was written in a mix of classical French and Latin which had been bequeathed to me by my Dark Master some years ago. Its age meant the spine would not have held the book together if it hadn't been reinforced by a black leather binding on its spine which was steadily greying as the book itself aged. But it was still in a passable condition and thus good enough for conducting magickal rituals with. I cherished this book as the gateway towards the Acausal Realm where the Dark Gods resided. But only those brave and noble souls with a heart of iron could venture into this realm without destroying their sanity for the Sinister Forces remained always unpredictable, inhuman (or more correctly, un-human) and incomprehensible to those who only operate from within the realm of the Causal, that is, the material realm of linear causality and classical logic. But the Acausal was not this, indeed it was a chaotic and demonic force. Above all, it was Sinister.

So I left the Magister Book in the safe-lock behind the mini-fridge and punched in my safety code: 1940. Then, I took a look outside from my balcony out to the streets below. I stood there for a while, looking down at everything below along Bourbon Street. It had stopped raining some minutes ago and the noisy chatter of the crowd could still be heard from the 4th floor of this hotel. I placed a cigar on my mouth and lit it up. As I inhaled the smoke and exhaled,

a soft jazz tune could be heard from below as the laughter of mundanes irritated my ears before. I decided to turn back inside my room and doze off for the day. I'd be meeting Seamus tomorrow.

SEAMUS

"Well there you are Henri!" he called out to me as I made my way inconspicuously into the bar. It was Seamus.

He walked up to me with a steady gate, a cigar in his hand and a glass in the other.

"How goes?" I asked him.

"Fucking great, its Mardi Gras!"

We sat by the bar at a table of our own while a waitress came over from behind the bar counter and asked us, "what can I get you guys?"

"Just some beer," Seamus responded as he took his sunglasses off him.

It was still only the evening but the bar was already getting stacked with people. The waitress left us and came back two minutes later with a pitcher of Irish Guinness. Seamus poured himself a glass and took a few sips from it.

He'd sported a recently grown moustache, different from his clean-shaven look from the last time I saw him. Seeing that he was constantly on the run from the FBI, I was not surprised in the least with his new disguise of a moustache-spouting, sun-glass wearing, hard-drinking lout. Seamus needed to fit in, especially with all the drunkards in town.

He came to New Orleans from Mobile to sell me the weapons I would need to carry out my massacre and I trusted him with getting me the best equipment possible. Seamus was, out of all things a pro-Confederate Creole Southerner and war-vet who had been discharged from the Army some years ago and had formed his own gang of travelling marauders with his old comrades from his Army days after returning from Iraq. He told me a few of his stories.

"Man, I just recently came back from Montreal. It was the greatest fucking thing!" he told me as he drank a bit more from his glass.

"I'd been invited up by this Asian-American called Lucas something, forgot his name, and his Pakistani buddy Nasir. Lucas was probably some ninja or something. He was pretty nuts. So I bought up some of my old war buddies to see what kind of hell we could unleash there."

He talked about what had occurred in Montreal while he was there, "That Pakistani guy though, he was some Zoroastrian. He kept on blabbering on about an 'Islam without Islam' or some kind of crap like that. But this Nasir guy, boy, what a crazed mullah! He convinced everyone he was some Mad Wizard who could conjure up demons and shit. He told me he had a jinn looking out for him which he consulted for some dark magick shit. It was an incredible week of just fucking mayhem!"

It had to be said, Seamus led an interesting double-life as an arms dealer and a mercenary. I liked his drunken tales that he would routinely tell me whenever we met at a bar.

"There was also this Satanic biker, his name was Victor. He came up from Texas with his own biker gang alongside him. But I got to tell ya, Henri, we made some hell up in Montreal! Killed a bunch of fucking SJWs, feminists, hipsters, faggots, every motherfucker we killed those sons of bitches on the spot! They called us, 'the Awesome Foursome'!"

It made a great story, and the last time I heard from them, this "Awesome Foursome" had apparently massacred up to 100 000 people up in Montreal in just a week's time. Things were getting crazier and this was just the start of it all.

My own plans were to harness the forces of destruction in the Causal Realm for Sinister ends and aid it in its goal of upsetting the materialist Magian Order. It was a Faustian bargain to the end, a Devil's Deal. But the Sinister forces could not be placated except with more daring acts of terror and more sacrifices of opfers, that is, useless morons, to the Dark Gods. We were to be its agents in this material realm, in the realm of the Causal.

Unfortunately, some agents of Chaos were unaware that their own acts aided and nourished Chaos and thus were far too undisciplined to truly harness it for Sinister ends. But we who were consciously agents of Chaos, who sought to fulfill the mission of Chaos, could harness and comprehend it even though we could never totally control it. But this made our own powers, not just stronger than the undisciplined, but also more directed and yes, disciplined. To wage war against the forces of Order would be to bring us to the next goal of the Sinister Dialectic, to physically manifest the Acausal from out of the Causal. Acts of terror would aid this process, as they surely were at this moment of social rapture.

"You've got the guns and stuff, Seamus?" I asked him in a quiet tone as he finished his glass of beer.

"Yeah, I've got it Henri. It's in the back. Come, I'll show you it."

We left some tips on our table as we left the bar. Making our way across a hall-way jammed with people of all sorts, we went down the stairs to the streets beneath. Seamus and I crossed the rose-decorated promenade as the Mardi-Gras floats passed us by as we heard live jazz music playing outside while the jeering and cheering of the crowd outside seem to fill up the damp, wet air with noisy chatter. All of this would be replaced with scenes of terror and chaos in the days that would come…

Seamus led me down the streets of the French Quarter as we walked against the massive crowds that had formed outside to see the floats floating by as musicians and dancers on top performed to the pleasure of the crowd. The crowd became more jubilant as the minutes passed. Their audacious and stupendous behavior could only become more and more ridiculous. I had had it with their outlandish costumes, colorful dresses and ridiculous make-up which only made the situation that much more surreal. It was as if none of the mundanes here understood what would happen here in just a few days' time. But I did not let this bother me; I needed my weapons first before I could even begin my slaughter.

"Well here we are!" he said as we stopped by a dirty, empty alleyway whose sole occupants were dumps of garbage and where Seamus had parked his '94 Chevy SUV.

"Just hold on a sec, I've got your gear in the trunk."

With a little shove, Seamus clicked open the back of his trunk with his hands. And there it was, stored behind the trunk were boxes of ammunition, a HK-416 battle rifle, a S&W revolver and batches of grenades. He also had Kevlar vests with him.

"Voila! A fucking arsenal for your own little private army!" he declared as he showed me his goods.

He picked up the HK-416 and posed with it with a lighted cigar in his mouth which he took from out his pocket.

"I had one of these sons-of-bitches when I was in Iraq! I reckon I killed a few people with it!"

"This is exactly what I needed Seamus." I told him.

"You betcha!" exclaimed Seamus, "I stole all of this from under their nose before I got discharged from the Army!"

Seamus was beaming about how he managed to get his hands on such weaponry.

"Man, you can't imagine how idiotic the Army can be sometimes! They left all this sick equipment just lying there on the floor. It was just ripe for the taking, so I took it from them!"

He laughed as he told me this, his voice gave away his sense of pride in having literally screwed the Army over for some rather expensive equipment.

"How much for the whole thing?" I inquired.

"$45 000!" responded Seamus.

"I've got that amount", I told him, "I'll automatically deposit you the money in two days' time."

"Of course you will! Or else me coming up here would have been a waste of time."

Before he left in his SUV, there was still one question I needed to ask from him.

"Seamus, this massacre is going down regardless of any personal preferences. The Sinister forces have proclaimed it necessary and their will is my own," I said as I tried to explain to him my plans.

"I need your support," I told him, "come with me to make hell tomorrow."

"Well hell, Henri! You know I've always got your back!"

"So are you in or out?" I asked

"Of course I'm in!" answered Seamus, "I'll see you tomorrow then. We'll make hell, like old times!"

Before he left for good, he helped me pack up the gear I would need for tomorrow's massacre. We placed everything within a secured and reinforced black gun case. We then covered it with duct tape and placed it on a trolley and covered it with Seamus' black trench-coat. Seamus then drove me down to my hotel and helped me move the gear up to my room. It took us just 15 minutes and, fortunately, we did not arouse the suspicions of the hotel staff or guests. They seemed to all assume we were regular guests at the hotel. That would cost them their lives tomorrow…

THE RITUAL

For the rest of the day, I scouted out the entirety of the French Quarter and found out the paths the police did for their regular patrols as well as which areas were the most densely populated

and at which time of the day. The strategy was simple: First, eliminate the police and then focus on the civilians.

However, I still had not a clue what Seamus would be doing. He had just left without giving me an indication of what role he would play in tomorrow's massacre but I trusted in his reliability. Perhaps, he would show up tomorrow with his gang of marauders! That would be a welcome relief!

As the day turned to night, I finally returned to my hotel in order to prepare for the next day's glorious events. Back at my room, I unsealed the gun case of duct tape and opened it up, removing the contents of the gun case one by one. First were the magazines which already contained rounds in them. Seamus had given me nine magazines, each of them already loaded. Then, grabbing the HK-416 from out of the gun case, I lifted it up and took a glance at it. It was still new and had a nice, shiny luster to it. The handling was also good and didn't have any excess weight that would make it unwieldy during a firefight. Overall, this could not have been a better choice of a weapon. Second was the revolver which I weighed with both of my hands. This one was a regular police-issue revolver that seemed to date from the 70s but, as Seamus had once told me, was still a reliable gun. I placed some rounds in the wheel and then clamped it shut, placing it in my holster for later use. Then, I took out the Kevlar vest and placed it on the floor. Finally, there were the grenades. Seamus had given me ten of them in total. Luckily for me, I had a grenade belt which I latched the grenades onto. With this gear, I was ready for some mass-killing. I only had one more thing left that I had to do….to meditate.

So I walked towards the lock where I had left the "Magister" book by itself. After unlocking it, I took out the "Magister" book which had been safely left in there untampered and I placed it on the floor as I prepared myself for a ritual which would cleanse me of any remaining doubts as I prepared myself spiritually and physically for tomorrow's culling. Taking out my two candles, I placed them onto a stand and lit both candles before carefully placing them both on the floor. I also grabbed my knife and made an incision on my palm, blood oozing out. I used the blood and painted it over my forehead and eyebrows with my own blood. Then, kneeling down, I opened the "Magister" book to the chapter concerning ritual sacrifice and began the chants as I cleared my mind of any more doubts and hesitations that would prevent me from actualizing tomorrow's events.

By chanting in both Latin and French with my eyes closed, I gradually managed to purge my mind of any more doubts. Actually, the whole ritual was quite soothing to my mind and gave me the spiritual strength that would be needed for tomorrow's glorious massacre. For this, I chanted for 25 minutes in repetition, the chanting becoming ever more intense until finally I was in a state of deep meditation. I remained in this state for what seemed like an eternity before I awoken. I had a vision while I was in deep meditation.

The vision showed me my fate tomorrow, indicating to me that I would die a hero's death. A dark, demonic figure with a flowing black cloak had appeared to me. The cloak he was

wearing then suddenly morphed into a pair of bat-like wings as he then flew across a city with many people beneath. It looked exactly like New Orleans, the French Quarter to be exact. I saw him throwing orbs of fireballs that turned into an inferno as it hit the ground and burned the people beneath as terror struck the hearts of the mundanes below. I could hear him laughing in a most diabolical way. As he flew across the city, continuously throwing these fireballs at the mundanes beneath, enflamed bodies were running to and fro as they tried to escape this creature's aerial bombing. He would fly in sharp angles, dive down and then suddenly pull up again into the air as he made some intense circling movements across the city skies above. And just as quickly as he moved through the skies, in an instant, he had landed on top of me with a sudden *oompf!* as his sharp claws dug deep into my chest. Strangely, it was painless. He looked me straight in the face but I couldn't make out his face which seemed to be, oddly, completely faceless. Yet, a slithering snake-like tongue protruded from out of his faceless head. And he told me this in a snake-like way, "thousanddsssss…… Noctuliusssss!"

And just as suddenly as he had appeared, he then flew away. But where he had stood with his claws penetrating my chest, there was blood leaking out from out of my chest. Then, seeming to be fainting away, I suddenly awakened! With my fate now clear to me, I gradually regained my composure and got up. Now, I understood everything.

With this vision, I understood that the casualties would number in the hundreds if not in the thousands! Gladdened by this news but also realizing that this meant inevitable death in the process, my will resolved itself to fulfilling the goals of the Sinister dialectic as tomorrow's culling got underway. With my fate understood, I accepted my will as that of the will of the Dark Gods and of the Acausal forces beyond and yonder!!

THE MASSACRE

I awoke the next morning to the sound of massive explosions in the background which startled me as much as it had awakened me. It seemed the culling had already started without me! So I got out of bed and grabbed my gear, donning my Kevlar chest over my chest as I ran towards the door and out into the hallway. I took the stairway beside my room as I ran quickly ran down the whole flight of stairs from the 4th floor down to the ground floor. I was met with a scene of carnage at the reception room as I saw tourists retreating back into the hotel, tripping over themselves as they ran for shelter from whatever was going on outside. To cause some havoc, I shot a valet, it was the same valet who had helped with my suitcase, in the chest with my HK-416 with a three-shot burst and then switched to auto and mowed down a group of tourists right by the entrance. I then shot at another person who had sat down by a sofa near the hallway leading to the elevators. He was lying down, bleeding profusely. I ended his life with a shot to his head with my revolver.

Bang!

But I needed to make my way outside, so I blew out the entrance doors with my rifle and kicked it open. As I came outside, I was met with the most awesome scene of carnage yet to befall a city…

Explosions were still going from a distance as a terrified crowd was running away from the scene of the explosions. A massive stampede had commenced as people tripped over and ran over each other as they tried to flee to safety. Many people were crushed in this ensuing mayhem, adding to casualties that I no longer needed to waste with my ammunition. To add the chaotic confusion, I threw a grenade into this crowd as they fled from the direction that they had been running from.

BOMPF!!!!! went the grenade as a splash of blood decorated the air with the limbs of the many mundanes as their limbs fell down to the ground. Today, it was literally raining human limbs!

Some of those who weren't killed by the initial blast, I shot them in the face as they tried to reach out to me with their arms. All I could muster to say to them was, "your time is up!" before I shot them in the face. A woman was crawling along the streets with her intestines blown out as she moaned and cried out for help. She was missing both legs and was covered in her own blood and that of others. To end her pathetic life, I curb-stomped her head onto the pavement with my boots as her brain matter came out of her skull, sticking to my boot. To clean the mess she had made, I detached her jaw from her face with my bare hands and used it to wipe clean the sole of my boot. I needed to stay clean as I performed this 'surgical procedure' among the many mundanes. After all, culling was a medical procedure.

Walking past all the screaming and terrified people, I moved towards the opposite direction from where they were running away from to see what exactly was going on over there. Some of the mundanes seemed to ignore me, others I shot down as I moved past them. However, some police officers had caught up to me and were firing at me from the balconies of some of the buildings. I took cover behind a car on the street and fired back with my HK-416. The cops were overpowered by me though, and I killed all three of them. I shot one at the neck as he fell off the balcony and onto the street below. The other had come from around the corner of the building in front of me and I shot him point-blank in the chest before I shot off his jaw as he laid on the ground. The last cop I shot had tried to run away to safer cover but I got a shot at him from behind.

Blat blat blat!!!!

He was dead before he even knew it.

I reloaded my rifle as my walk broke into a run as I made my way towards the scene of the explosions. As I did, I suddenly saw, to my own surprise, a Blackhawk helicopter was coming over from across the skies above. It was making some crazy maneuvers in the air and flying quite low as it turned around and made another strafe across the city as I saw machine-gun fire coming from out of its side. I could make out that the Blackhawk was marked on both sides with the Confederate Flag. It was then, that I realized that it was Seamus. Seamus was on top of a Blackhawk helicopter (I had no clue how he had acquired it, probably stolen it from the Army).

As I looked up, I could see Seamus was sitting on his chopper, and firing at the crowd beneath with a mini-gun that was attached to a MG pod mounted to the side of the Blackhawk. Wagner's "the Valkyries" was blaring from out of its loudspeakers as Seamus fired round after round of ammunition into the crowd below. In truth, the mix of the Blackhawk from above firing mg rounds at the mundanes below to Wagner's "the Valkyries" was truly a terrifying ordeal to experience for anyone involved, particularly for the mundanes below. It seemed that each mg round he fired seemed to match the note of the song as Seamus methodically shot at everyone and everything he could see. It was then, that I knew Seamus had not abandoned me to my fate. Indeed, he wanted to outdo me.

"You want some of this, you motherfuckers!!!! Fuck y'all!!!" he screamed as his mg rounds ripped through the New Orleans sky.

Seamus was wearing a pilot's helmet and had combat gloves on as well as an airman's goggles. The Blackhawk was piloted by one of his army buddies as they wreaked havoc from above as I did so from below. He was covering me from the air with his chopper.

"YEEEHAAWWWWW," he cried out, "if these were a bunch of iraqis they'd call me a fucking racist but this MG is an equal-opportunity killer!!!!" yelled Seamus as he fired again and again.

He then flew across to the police station and took out a RPG from out of nowhere and fired it into the police station. The police there had no chance, armed as they were, only with pistols. Many of them were incinerated from the explosion and the surviving ones were blown up again when Seamus fired another RPG round at them, this time targeting the police cars parked outside the police station. The cops taking over behind their cops cars died in the ensuing explosion or were crushed by their own cars.

"FUCK DA POLICE!!!! You muthafuckas gave me a ticket for illegal parking, so I blow you up!!!" Seamus yelled as he slaughtered the cops from above.

"The Confederacy is back and BIGGER and BADDER than ever!!!!" he declared from his loudspeaker.

"We are taking over New Orleans and you motherfuckers better raise the Confederate Flag or we'll kill you!!!!"

Seamus made another strafe around as he spotted me below.

"Oh hey Henri! How ya doing down there???" he said to me.

I yelled back at him, "I'm doing great! Keep this up and this might just be the culling we want!"

"I am thoroughly enjoying this culling!" he responded.

He then flew away again, firing from his mg as he did so. His chopper was still blaring 'the Valkyries' from out of its loudspeakers.

As I looked around me, I finally realized just how much carnage we had done. Hundreds if not thousands of corpses were strewn all over the streets of the French Quarter, many with their limbs detached from their bodies. Pools of blood were pouring down the sidewalks and into the drainage below. I reloaded again and made my way methodologically through the corpses checking to see if any were still alive.

Seamus had managed to kill off the majority of the cops with his attack on the police station but there was no doubt that more cops would arrive

at this scene of carnage. I saw a cop, dazed and confused walking towards me. His uniform was covered in debris. I pointed my rifle at him.

"Hey, don't shoot me. Please. I'm….I'm just doing my job. Please."

Splat!

He fell knee first onto the cold pavement below when I pulled the trigger of my revolver. But he was still alive, clutching his stomach with his hands where I had shot him. So I unsheathed my bayonet and came over to his side, then with a move of my knife I slit his throat from behind and decapitated him with one slice of my knife. I removed his head and threw it down the street. It hit the hard pavement with a *clunk!* Then I sat down to recollect myself and reloaded my rifle.

But this peace was not to last for the SWAT team had arrived in their armored trucks some five minutes later armed with M-4 carbines and shotguns, ready to deal with me. So I hid beneath a car, and throw a grenade at their line of sight as they made their way down the streets, one-by-one with rifles pointed.

BOOPF!!!!

The grenade went off and injured or maimed some of the members of the SWAT team. There were about eight of them and I managed to kill four of them with my grenade. They hadn't seen it coming. So I took aim again and engaged in a firefight with the remaining four who took shelter behind their armored trucks.

It was then, that Seamus returned again in his Blackhawk chopper, ready to make hell again. He threw a grenade from out of the side of his chopper and down below at the four remaining SWAT team members, killing the two hiding behind their armored trucks and crushing the other when the truck flipped over and crushed his chest. The last remaining SWAT member, I picked off with my rifle.

However, just as we had eliminated this SWAT team, three new SWAT teams converged at our site in their armored trucks. They had me surrounded. Having been encircled, they began aggressively firing at me with their rifles. One of their shots hit my chest and then another. But I was still alive. The Kevlar vest had protected me.

So I ran back towards them, fired and fired again with my rifle. I didn't hit any of them this time but I saw Seamus come back in his chopper yet again. This seemed to intimidate the SWAT officers as some of them ran away. Seamus then fired his mg at them which zipped through the air at such a rapid rate that it took just seconds for him to basically annihilate them.

He called out to me form his loudspeakers, "How ya doing Henri?!?!"

"I'm good! We just have to keep this up!"

"Hell yeah!!!" Seamus enthusiastically responded.

But our luck was not to last, because as soon as Seamus had said that. We realized that the government had sent in the National Guard and the Army and their soldiers who were armed to the teeth to deal with us. An APC disembarked its heavily armed soldiers behind us. Seamus disengaged from then and flew away towards the combat choppers that were also heading our way. They had decided to send in the whole army to deal with just two guys, showing how desperate they had gotten…

"Holy shit Seamus!" I called out to him.

"This isn't anything that we can't handle! The Dark Lords are here with us today, testing our willpower and determination! So let's give them hell!"

This was to be our last stand.

So I lobbed the last remaining grenades at the soldiers who were coming towards me. A few of them were killed, the rest I managed to suppress with a concentrated spray of fire from my rifle. The APC then moved forward and aimed its turret at me, but just as it did, it suddenly exploded!

Seamus had suddenly flew over again and his chopper had shot a missile at it from its weapons cache, blowing up the APC as a result. It seemed that Seamus' had gotten his hands on a special version of the Blackhawk that could transform itself to an 'attack' mode which equipped it with lock-on missiles.

"This Blackhawk is a beast!" said Seamus over the loudspeakers.

"I stole this from Area-51 as a truth-or-dare thing with my old Army buddies. And what did you know?!?!? The government had been developing some new Blackhawk prototypes!"

He then rotated his mg around and replaced it with a grenade launcher which he used to engage the soldiers below who returned fire. Some of them had gathered at the roofs of the buildings to shoot a RPG round at Seamus. Luckily, he managed to do some evasive maneuvers away from them before he shot another volley of rockets at this group of soldiers on top. But his chopper had been damaged from the firefight, even though it also had reinforced armored plating, but it was also probably heavily damaged from the dogfight in the air against the attack helicopters that were still coming our way.

"I think this is it, Henri! It was good fighting alongside you!" he said as he saluted to me below.

"It was my pleasure!" I called out to him.

As we did so, we realized that this really was it. Seamus disengaged again and flew away from the troops coming towards us as I jammed in my last round. I could hear some screaming far away and some explosions. I reckoned that Seamus had decided to fly off to massacre a few more civilians before he was shot down. I admired his commitment to the culling. But I had to stand my ground.

I could hear the soldiers approaching me. So I yelled out to them, "I'm here! Just shoot me!"

My Kevlar chest was of no use anymore after the battering it took from the SWAT team and I had sustained some severe wounds around my chest area.

They yelled back at me, "drop your gun then!"

I didn't. Instead, I sprung up and began firing back at them but I was met with a heavy volley of rifle fire as they managed to take me down. I was then lying on the ground bleeding from out of my chest as these soldiers came towards me. They pointed their rifles at my face, ready to execute me.

But just as they did, I saw Seamus flying towards me again rapidly throwing grenade after grenade at everything below. destroying everything beneath him. I could just make out his face, which showed the most sinister and diabolical expression I had ever seen. His sharp tongue was out of his mouth and he had the meanest scowl that was humanly possible as he lodged grenade after grenade like bombs on the people below. He was screaming, howling and yelling all sorts of profanities as he came towards me in his Blackhawk. Seamus was my devil in the air, having come to save me at the very last moment. This had just distracted the soldiers enough that they began returning fire at Seamus.

"IF I'M GOING TO DIE, THEN I'M TALKING ALL YOU MUTHAFUCKERS WITH ME!!!" he yelled.

His chopper had a trail of smoke coming from out of its tail. It was quickly making a descent towards them at a high velocity, indeed, Seamus was making a nose-dive towards this group of soldiers. He planned on taking everyone with him as his final sinister act. As this happened, some of the soldiers fired back at him again.

Just as he was about to crash into us, he screamed, "HAIL DEATH! GLORIOUS VANQUISHER OF ALL MEDIOCRITY!!!"

I could hear Seamus yelling as his chopper came down fast towards us from above the skies as it came crashing towards the ground and crushing those soldiers beneath him as the now flaming chassis of the helicopter came hurtling towards me with its rotor slicing apart the limbs of the remaining soldiers. It was heading towards me at a great velocity and then, I closed my eyes, accepting my inevitable fate as the Seamus' chopper came crashing towards me….

SPLURCK!!!

Oh, Darkness…here I am.

THE ART OF

ERICA FREVEL

TIAMAT ALTAT PIECE

TOTAL DESTRUCTION OF THE CITIES OF MEN

THE PACT

UNDERBELLY – An Insight Role

Disclaimer: For security reasons and out of respect for certain individuals, some details are left out. My actual friends and comrades have been erased for their own sake.

A few years back I became a drug dealer for about two and a half years, thus experiencing a nerve-wracking way of life and experiencing chaotic situations, learning extremely important lessons in life, becoming more street-wise, facing many threats and dangers; and ultimately discarding that lifestyle altogether.

Although not one of the classical Insight roles, this period certainly had all the characteristics; I pretty much left behind and sacrificed my normal mundane existence of the time, leaving my college, having no job, not paying taxes, distancing myself from society, family and friends, changing my views completely, even sometimes forcing myself to play a persona who was the complete opposite of my character, keeping my satanic and spiritual views secret (to an extent that I almost forgot about them), facing real risks, threats and dangers every day, even being assaulted a couple of times. I did not use a bank or ID at that time, I could get almost everything I needed through black market or underground channels. Even my residence was a black market rent. This time of my life changed me for the better, hardened my spirit and made my true character more clear and sharp.

At a fairly young age I got interested in intoxicating substances and hallucinogens in particular. Before I had the chance to experiment with them, I studied them as much as I could with much enthusiasm. Later, when I started experimenting on myself I slowly became and expert of drugs, their effects and history. A couple of years would pass until I ultimately made the leap to a full time drug dealer and enthusiast.

At that time I found drugs to be enjoyable, and like most I started to use them to escape the intolerable oppression of modernity, and to ease some unresolved pain and issues; being incredibly dishonest with myself and quite frankly foolish and weak in character. I foolishly sought the easy way out; which I later found to be the worst way out.

I used drugs. I tried all the drugs I could get my hands on; every time seeing more, meeting more people involved in the trade of drugs, finding it an interesting sport and profession. As the couple of years went by my determination to experience this lifestyle surfaced completely. In my subconscious I had made the decision, regardless of my worries of what my family and friends might think or do. So, one day I did. I turned on, tuned in and dropped out.

At the beginning there was a genuine feeling of excitement, freedom, danger and anticipation; a liberation I had been waiting for. I can still feel that feeling that day when I made the leap. I recall the sheer excitement and danger. It felt good. It felt sinister. I felt this was my destiny unfolding. Not for a lifetime, but for a time; that particular time in my life had come. I sought out an individual who I knew was into these things, and who I knew was eager to make money from selling drugs; believing the false illusion of the rich, happy drug dealer. He had made some connections, but lacked the money to buy the amount needed for profit. One day; the very same day I left my college, we got into his car and went to meet some individual who would sell us 200 grams of marijuana, to begin our adventures. To fund this heresy I used the inherited savings from my father, who hanged himself when I was a youngster. Having many unresolved, underlying issues regarding that matter, I was not influenced by greed or a desire for money; I was fueled by anger; driven by rage.

I simply could not do it to myself to finish college, serve the system and the ideals and rules of others, to do what I did not believe in; it was impossible for me. I had to learn from experience. I *had* to know the edges of life. I had to live in a way that would penetrate my numbness. I did the opposite of what was being advised to me. I did the opposite of what I was taught as a child. I did the utterly satanic thing. So I turned my back on the mundane, the comfort, the illusions and begun my short lived life of crime and danger.

As we started, it did not take long for me to notice the pathetic behavioral patterns of people. They would come flocking to us like leeches; like flies. Pretending to be friends, pretending to be interested in something other than drugs. Pretending, pretending, pretending. The day started with drugs, it ended with drugs. There was no partaking in the forgotten socio-economical illusory goo. There was no watching

of tv, no paying of taxes. There was an actual living in an actual underworld. It went nicely at first, phone was ringing, customers were acquired, connections were made. Marijuana, cocaine, amphetamine; what could go wrong with such 'bliss'?

For months we sold marijuana, gaining money, influence and connections. Seemingly innocent and promising. At that time there was an uprising; a surge of something classical, a fad, an obsession among the customers. Something I had sworn never to get into; it was the little pink fuckers. It was 'ecstasy'. I can never forget this period. As I tried it, I foolishly decided it would be a good idea to please the customers and make some money with this newly found marvel.

This is where things got serious. As I was purchasing large amounts of ecstasy, I met increasingly more shady people, saw and heard of more serious things; assault, robbery, rape, murder. I got more removed from reality myself due to the consumption of ecstasy and increasingly more amounts of amphetamines and cocaine. It felt purely chaotic. Purely out of control, purely blissful; purely confident. In my drug induced frenzy I did not realize the risks I was taking. After we had sold the first 100 tablets, I took it upon myself to start my own venture; called my buddies and told them it was over, I was taking it all on me. The paranoia was immense at the time. I expected a SWAT team breaking into my residence any time. The police were actually driving in circles around my home during daytime. I was intimidated by the big, bad drug dealers, I expected their henchmen to come and stab and rob me anytime. I did not recognize myself in the mirror.

As it came to purchasing the next batch of ecstasy tablets, my long lost uncle (Opfer candidate no. 1) contacted me. Somehow having heard of my large amounts of money and drugs; my crazed antics and minute success, he offered me the very best ecstasy tablets and protection from others in the trade. At the time organized biker gangs such as 'Outlaws' and 'Hells Angels' were becoming more prominent, taking over the underbelly, recruiting people to their clubs, and selling synthetic, cheap, fake and dangerous new substances. I remember meeting a guy in town who was recruiting people into a supporter club for one of the gangs, and being the satanist I am, I was smart enough to stay out of that pathetic shit, subconsciously knowing my venture in these fields would eventually come to an end; and obviously never partaking in any sort of group mentality.

So, I met this uncle of mine (Opfer candidate no. 1) to get 300 tablets of a new type of ecstasy cocktail. I remember waiting in his car, seeing how far off he was in his drug-haze, barely talking, driving from one spot to another. I felt a little over my head, listening to him talk in his phone; I remembered how far off I was from my true character and potential, and I feared I was closing in to a new low. We waited for hours. The guy was late. And simply because my uncle was late for dinner with his wife because of all this; he had the poor guy put in a trunk of a car, driven to a specific location, then driving there himself, leaving the car and beating the guy down, breaking his ribs, leg and arm, then

leaving him on the parking lot. All with me present as some sort of "silent power display". That incident even came on the news few hours later. I went home with 300 ecstasy tablets. It was at that time I started realizing how far I had come. How wrong I was to myself. What heresy I was conducting.

I remember one incident after this where me and my 'friends' were at my home playing music pretty loud, and the police knocking on the door. They had got a complaint about loud noises, and thus could enter the premises. So they did, and the rats of course ran away like puny cowards, leaving me to explain all to the cops. So I did; I told them we were just going out to the town, and would stop the music now. On my living room table were rolled up bank notes, and clear evidence of cocaine. There was cash here and there; clearly not the residence of a law-abiding tax-paying citizen. Under the table however, there were the now ~250 ecstasy tablets, and another 100 grams of marijuana. What the officer did was to point at a bottle of moonshine standing proudly on the table and ask me: "what is this?" and I answered: "this is vodka". Then he wrote down my name, phone number and miraculously left. Had he found the ecstasy tablets I could have been charged with attempted murder and put to prison for up to 7 years. Realizing all this, and the simple fact that the rats had ran like the pathetic useless scum they really are, I was deep in. I was alone.

I was no longer with my 'buddies' in this. My family had completely stopped trying to communicate with me. My actual friends were far and gone. I was on my own. I was on the edge.

The true, very, actual edge. There were police on one side. There were biker gangs on the other side. There was possible death on the third side. I continued. I gave in. My customers were now more impersonal, ranging from 15 year old girls to 50 year old men with missing teeth. I was in the wrongest place. The darkest, lowest place. I was meeting the more prominent criminals for new batches, the big bad ones.

It surprised me how little these people actually knew about drugs, and I found their general ignorance disappointing to say the least. I guess I expected more individuals like myself; with a hidden, higher, satanic goal of learning in life; with at least more or equal knowledge of substances and chemicals like I had. But I never met even one. These criminals were worthless, pathetic scum, who obviously had unresolved issues from their own past or childhood, and knowing this I felt stupid and foolish, being around these dangerous, unpredictable insects. My age old anger came back. Now directed at myself, for having started this in the first place; I had done this to myself. My body was alerting me, my true friends had gone, my family had given up, and now; finally, I had learned. I had felt, I had lived

Many things happened, many things I did which I can never disclose publicly, and some of which I can never tell anyone. The broad picture is that of the whole period itself; of the role which I undertook. In all this there came a time of truth, a time where I simply had to stop and rethink my strategy. A time of remembering. When that time caught up to me, stopped using all the drugs on myself, let alone sell them; I stopped

communicating with any and all people involved with this now worthless sport. I discarded it all. I threw it away. I had now known it, tried it all. If I really cared for myself this was the time to stop, as it was. It took a few months to recover physically, about one year psychologically. I isolated myself further. I discarded the people who were involved in any way with the trade of drugs. I distanced myself even further from the mundane and the Magian. I became a Hermit of sorts.

One calm, cold, dark winter night I took a walk through my neighbourhood at the time, and I remember seeing the stars, Venus, and the Moon, some aurora borealis, and of course feeling the cold, relentless, clear, honest air. At that time I realized what I had done, what I had lived. A smile was unavoidable; my satanic, spiritual, esoteric attitude had awakened from it's nap. I felt it. What I had done was utterly sinister, satanic and successful. There were no consequences to be faced other than the painful and intense experience itself. I had completed something. I had been someone other than myself, and now I was myself again. The cold, black sky of stars, Venus shining, Moon staring; reminded me of the higher goal I had so foolishly forgotten. And I smiled to myself. I felt it. I had lived it. The trees saw me standing there. I greeted them once more.

And I felt liberated. Alone. New. I had not only discarded my own painful childhood, but also the choices I had made trying to deal with that childhood, and now somehow I managed to survive an unsaid catastrophe and smile to the moon, a new man, hardened by fear and feared by the fearful; I had become the very thing I myself had feared before. There was nothing that could threat me now. I smiled – I still smile – O, the irony that is life. O, what it takes now to put me out of balance is too great for any individual to undertake. O, that which can persuade me now must be of the gods, or else it is not even worth my attention. O, the irony; the sinister truth. I had fulfilled the beginnings of my Destiny.

As the said hermit I started pursuing my original goals again, as if I had never done anything other. I took up the gift of meditation once again, which was given to me at a very young age, liberating me from the shackles of the putrid magian, Nazarene infectious disease completely. I meditated, I created art, I composed music, I wrote, I remembered, I vibrated the truth into my own mind. And the profound experiences from that time rendered all mind-altering substances obsolete. Even the strong effects of hallucinogens such as deliriants, DMT and psychedelic mushrooms. There was simply more. It was piercing; there was no running away from it, it was there and it had nothing to do with any substance known to man. What was the point of taking a substance when such immense energies can me made manifest and experienced with breath alone?

I became. I felt as if emerging from pupae. I was me. I was again the same small boy who dreamed of demons, a dark blue sky, yellow stars, and the silent trees watching and dancing in the wind. I felt more. I felt myself. O the putrid human failures. The war on drugs is not only a failure; it is a hoax. We live in a world of depraved lies,

sick illusions and utter weakness. Your opinions are not going to fight a war for you. Only you can do so yourself with your own unique experience of life on the edge, in any manner that fits your Wyrd. The Magian must be destroyed. It must be discarded as we discard our own feces. We must destroy the modern, 'illuminated', putrid, sick, rotten, mundane, magian, worthless, unnatural infection. Remember the mountains in the night? Think of trees dancing in wind. See the stars on a snowy winter midnight. Commune with the acausal. Nature does not forget. Nature does not forgive. Stars remember and see. Stars need darkness to shine.

So, what was learned from this rebellious, seemingly pointless, heretical, dangerous way of life?

1) In itself this and any such adversarial way of life or 'insight role' will, 'if correctly understood', serve to strengthen, sharpen and make more clear, ones true, primordial and REAL character.

2) I have become more calm. I have become more sharpened in my own views. I have become truly proud of having purposefully endured pain, hatred, misery, worthlessness, and other negative forces. I am not afraid of the criminal underworld as the mundane is. I know who is who. I know what is what. I can see, I understand. I don't need help. I can fully understand an individual who is aspiring in that field, and I can sinisterly anticipate his demise; knowing that such a way of life has absolutely no future. I have completed crime 101. I know who is the real criminal. He wears a suit and a

tie, and bears a false inhuman smile on his false inhuman face.

3) Drugs, intoxicants and mind-altering substances have been rendered obsolete for me. A truly esoteric, occult, satanic or spiritual aspirant must come to find them to be distractions and abstractions from those experiences that are truly mystical, the 'true' and 'real' that most individuals undoubtedly fear; that which most individuals turn their backs on to give in to a return to illusions. "The hard way is the only way." The easy way is the way of the prey. 'Go hard or go home.'

4) Don't expect others to have equal or similar knowledge of the satanic, esoteric, spiritual or occult ways as you have. As the finding of such people is very rare, and as part of your own personal Wyrd, concentrate on your own personal learning; not the mundane opinions and worthless musings of other sentient beings. Listen instead to the whispers in the wind, look upon the dancing of the trees. Become one with Nature and walk through the black fires of the Abyss, or perish in foul submission.

Such was the simple way I learned and experienced the basic truths I hold on to. Not the truths of the Sinister Tradition; but rather the truths of the opposite: the sick. The inhuman: the rotten: the anti-cosmic. The enemy. And as so I strive to aspire, and to destroy the enemy at all costs. The times we live in are no ordinary times. These are the times of war, of truth and of culling.

Agios o Aosoth!

Yogesh Arya,
Iceland, 126 Y.F.

WORSHIP THE DARKNESS

Constantine Charagma

The Abyss is the one of the most common themes in occult literature. Without great surprise, it is also the most badly misunderstood. Whether you call it the Void, or the Hell, or the Great Darkness, the *Asat*, or the Primordial, it is all One. Absolute, eternal, and ceaseless in its desire to reincorporate us back into itself. It is at the center of everything, and it exists outside of time and space, as well as between time and space. Our limited intellect is unable to understand this directly through perception, and so it is only through the grace of gnosis – that is, whispers from the Void – that we are able to understand its supremacy and sublime nature.

The world we live in is an amalgamation of selfish whims and urges, given physical forms by the demigods – these are the demiurges, craftsmen, the jailers, the clever hands who have bound up our sentience within the three-dimensional prison we call existence. They are not evil, but they are selfish, in that they wish to maintain this false existence. They try to keep you trapped and confused, like a jealous lover who likes your company so much, that they decide to take you hostage, slash your tires, and lock you inside their house because they cannot stand to live without you. The demigods suffer from a psychosis, which compels them to isolate their own existence from the Abyss which wants – needs, really – to devour and consume them.

We are not meant to be here. We are meant to return to the Abyss, from which the demigods emerged. Mythology casts the Abyss as a hungry monster, but it is not so much *hungry* as it is *incomplete*. The gods, have left it, have stolen its divine essence and having forced the cosmos (and us) into existence – they have fractured the Unity of the Abyss, and so it seeks to reincorporate them, the cosmos, and us, back into its divine source. We must go back to godhead – that is, to the perfect unity that predates the brokenness of the cosmos.

The Abyss is not even our parent – it is more than that – it is our source. You are a piece of the Abyss, a shard of its divine unity. Now, we are now incomplete. We know, deep down inside, that this is not where we are meant to be. So to distract ourself from the pain of separation, we have created religions, myths, stories to justify our purposeless lives, lies to give this charade some kind of meaning.

There are many occult paths in this world, but most are false leads, dead-ends and alleys that were planted by the demigods. They cannot help you – not really. At most, they can assist you in obtaining momentary blessings or benefits, but they cannot truly help you ascend, because they do not WANT you to ascend. The only escape from this universe, this prison, is descent into the Abyss. This is easier than it ought to be, but harder than it sounds. Easy, because the Abyss wants you to return, and it wishes so bitterly to consume this universe and reclaim its wholeness. Hard, because as much as we might wish to return, our flesh is our jailer, a conspirator who struggles against our Abyssal urge. So we must learn to put the flesh to death, through its perversion, its discipline, its sublimation. The flesh can be overcome, and through sufficient punishment and austerity, what is at first a barrier to the Abyss can become the doorway through which the Abyss can enter this world.

If we are serious about escaping this prison, devotion is the only way, the only path. We must entirely submit to the Abyss, pray to it, sacrifice to it. Rites of blood and austerity are the most powerful tools of the path, through which we can allow the Abyss to consume us, our environments, and the cosmos itself.

The gods of mercy and kindness are liars, drug-peddlers and swindlers. They cover up our genuine suffering by masquerading as our friends and protectors. They are not. It is the dark gods, the spirits who have turned back to the Abyss, who are our real saviors. Those beings you call demons, fiends, monsters – they are the gods who have rejected the light of falsehood, and chosen to return to the Abyss. But because they are truly merciful, they seek to shatter this prison first. Whence we call them monsters and horrors and terrors, because they shatter the mundane prison, in the attempt to awaken the prisoners. When a spirit guides you to cut your flesh, it is saying "awaken". When it inflicts nightmares in the darkness of the night, it is whispering "wake up wake up wake up". When

these spirits slip inside you, hollow you out, and carry your soul back to the Void, they are not trying to hurt you. They are trying to liberate you from the lie that is the world around us. The spirits from the Void appear to torment us, because they are surgeons who are trying to cut through the muck and mire of the material world.

Sometimes, when the spirits feel the need to really intervene, to rescue a soul, they will attempt to possess someone. It is often an innocent, who does not deserve to be trapped in this world. When we see a person who is possessed by an Abyss spirit, they will often appear to be mad and raving, so we understand through gnosis that the soul is already gone – swallowed, by the Abyss. But the mind and the flesh remain, as the corpse is too perverse to die. We need to seek that level of spiritual advancement. Whiling living, we must seek to leave the flesh. Become the corpse. I do not say kill yourself, as that is stupidity. If you kill yourself while alive, you will merely be forced to take rebirth in another body. Some very wicked demigods use depression and illness to push people towards suicide, but this is a trick to prevent genuine gnosis. The true Abyssal Gnostic has so embodies the Void, that they have become the Living Dead. While living, their soul has gone on to Void realms, while the body continues to act and speak on auto-pilot. This is the true ascent, which is very difficult to describe, and harder yet to accomplish.

There once was a very holy Gnostic saint in New York, and she wanted very much to transcend the flesh. And so she prayed and prayed fervently for the spirits of the Void to possess her, hollow her out, and take her soul back to the Abyss. She began to have very strange dreams, which encouraged her to undertake bizarre rituals. She would fast on the new moon, burn her own hair soaked in her own blood as ritual offerings, and cut herself with pieces of jagged glass from the broken windows of a local church. She even took to sleeping in cemeteries, because (she reported) it was only there that she could hear the whispers of the Void clearly. Eventually she received the holy communion of unity (which cannot be described) – but then appeared to abandon all spiritual practices and to return to her regular professional life. Everyone commented on how 'normal' she seemed – except for her closest family and friends, who remarked that she was no longer "present" in the body. She would go about her day as if on autopilot – she worked, paid her taxes, and attended family events – but her conversations were all dull and insipid. Eventually, someone consulted with a psychologist, and after some attempts at therapy, the person was diagnosed with some severe dissociative disorder. Of course, the soul of the gnostic had ascended and gone back to the Abyss. The body and the mind had remained, and this is what the living family could not accept. But this saint is a great hero, and an example to us all.

Eventually, the soul of the saint did return, from the Abyss out of her great compassion for her family. Of course, by that time, her sense of compassion was really inhuman, and so she engaged in violent outbursts and acts of sexual transgression that left several people injured and

in need of counselling themselves. The saint, having shocked them out of their spiritually dead routines, died of an epileptic seizure shortly thereafter.

The rites and practices of the Ecclesia community, and other holy devotional societies such as the Tempel ov Blood and Res Satanae, are all intended to do one thing: to destroy the mortal, and unchain the immortal. The flesh is a trap by design, but it does not *need* to be a trap – it can be a doorway into terrible etheric realms. Through the abuse or indulgence of the flesh, it can be turned from a locked door into an open corridor. The anecdote above is an example of how the Abyss reaches out to us, seeking to consume us in its own quest for immortality. We seek to join it, it seeks to find us. The Abyss – our supersoul – seeks to consume us, we should ask to be consumed.

We may not have the courage or the dedication to enter the Abyss, but if we are willing to make steps towards the Abyss in this life, then we are assured that the spirits of the Abyss will take notice of our efforts, and seek to facilitate our better rebirth. Whether this is in a spiritual world that has already moved towards the Void, or within the Void itself, is unknown. But we must make the efforts to free ourselves of the demiurgic prison, as no one can do it for you otherwise.

Free yourself.

Worship the Darkness.

ENTITY

Constantine Charagma

When I was in college, I became very disillusioned with the Church, and I started to practice magic. Through luck (or misfortune), I discovered some strange dream rituals involving fasting, cutting, and blood offerings into several guttering candles, and this brought me into contact with a very powerful spirit from the Abyss. For reasons I will not get into here, I needed assistance, and It offered to help me, in exchange for my devotion and worship, and for carrying a lesser Abyssal entity with me. I agreed. Then, very strange things started to happen. First, they were happening to me, next to my family, then to the people I was friends with. It was like a spiritual sickness, and I was at the epicenter. The entity was using me as an anchor, and it seemed to grow stronger is it radiated further and further away. I knew it was hurting people, damaging relationships, eroding the community in which I lived, but it felt good. I liked the feeling of having a dark spirit coiled inside of me, lashing out at random. It was soothing, numbing even, in a strangely addictive kind of way. Sometimes, I would close my eyes and see through its eyes, and other times it would push my own consciousness aside and I would just be on autopilot while this Thing used me like a puppet. This happened at school mostly, it didn't normally take me over at home, since my parents would have been suspicious. The spirit would manifest when I was trying to sleep – it would shove my bed around, jolting me awake.

Or it would move the lamp beside my bed, shaking it gently, or making other objects move in the room by themselves. The entity was malicious, I could feel it clearly, but it did not want to hurt me in particular, and I afforded it the chance to hurt other people. I even took a particular comfort when it was there, like it was some hideous guardian angel.

Unfortunately, it did not limit itself to manifesting near me. My parents started to have frequent nightmares, and my little sister woke up one night screaming like an animal, shouting that the devil was in her room. I tried to explain to the entity that these kind of manifestations were bad for me, but either it did not understand, or perhaps it simply didn't care.

At school, though, that was where its power really shined. Somehow, this thing made me understand that it was able to hurt people, but I needed to direct it. I would envision lines of energy connecting me to people who I did not like – for example, there was this guy who was really into my girlfriend. So, I'd focus on him in class. I'd see the energy flowing between us, and I'd wish for the entity to travel along the line and to infect him. Sure enough, if I wished hard, then I'd see the weird reddish energy of the creature streaming out from me and into that fucker, and he'd start to get weak, or lethargic, or even sick in class. It became something of a game – class became an excuse to torment this person, and I think he somehow knew I was the one making him sick.

The downside was that the entity would jump to my friends as well. For some time, I had been trying to tell my best friend Patrick about this Aybssal entity and the weird things it was doing, and the weird black thoughts it was feeding my mind. He'd tell me it was all make-believe, wish fulfillment, stuff like that. So I asked the entity for a favor – I told it I wanted Pat to see what I was seeing, so I wouldn't think I was going crazy. Honestly, there were moments when I thought I was going crazy, but seeing the entity affecting other people, it reassured me that it wasn't all in my head. One weekend, my Patrick when to a party with his sister. It was a lousy party, so they decided to get some fresh air at the park up the street. To make a long story short, while they were chilling at the park, this Thing came out of the woods towards them, they said it looked like a spectral shape that was basically human, but bird-headed and with claws. It chased them all the way home, and when they locked themselves inside the house, it tried to get in through the upstairs window. My friend and his sister told me this, and then my friend asked me never again to try to send the entity to him again. I felt bad, because they were genuinely terrified, and his sister was hysterical when they told me about this misadventure.

Unfortunately, the one who suffered the most was my girlfriend at the time. She didn't quite believe me, but she did know that I wasn't mentally unstable, and so she tried to talk to a friend of hers who claimed to be a hereditary witch from a coven. Her friend said she wanted to meet me, and so my girlfriend arranged for us to meet at a party. That, to put it mildly, did not go well. When I got to the party, my girlfriend's friend was there – a tall, bony girl with a mop of unkempt hair. She looked nice enough, if cheaply dressed. However, when my girlfriend tried to introduce us, the Abyssal entity inside me reared up like an angry horse. People talk about a fight-or-flight reaction, and this was absolutely that. Part of me wanted to rape the girl, violate her there in front of all those people. Part of me wanted to leave, to escape being seen. For her part, when she saw me, her eyes grew a bit wild, and she told my girlfriend that she wanted to leave the party. Later that night, she called my girlfriend on the phone, and told her to break up with me. She said I was carrying a dangerous presence inside me, a shadowy entity with red eyes. My girlfriend didn't know what to think, but while they were talking, something started to scratch the underside of my girlfriend's bed, as if a cat or other clawed animal. My girlfriend was really afraid, since she didn't own any pets, and when she told the witch what was happening, the witch told her it was the entity, and it would only get worse with time.

My girlfriend gave me the choice to get help, or to end things with her. So we broke up. I rather liked her, but the entity didn't, and there was no sense in seeing her punished for distracting me from whatever agenda I was being steered towards.

This is the part of the story, where you'd think I'd get help from a priest or some local psychic.

But I'm not a victim or a faggot, or some dabbling Satanist. Despite the fact that I understood the entity was malicious, I enjoyed it. So when things got to the point that my friends and family were really freaking out, I simply left. I packed my things, and moved to another city. Eventually, I found a teacher, someone who understood spells and magic, and learned a few lessons – not on how to get rid of the entity, but how to merge with it, so it could never leave, and so I'd never be without it. Of course, at this point I wonder if maybe it intended all along for this to happen, or if it simply didn't care enough to resist when I intoned the spells to drill it into my bones and flesh. Either way, I no longer feel the presence of an external force inside me, I just feel myself like an alien presence inside of a human shell, and loose in the material world to play whatever awful games come to mind.

Now, I set my hand to writing the ritual that I discovered. It is very simple, but very difficult to do, and harder to undo if you don't like the rituals. If you are brave enough to call down the Abyss – to seek an audience with the Primordials who dwell there – then these steps might be of some use. This ritual is suitable for those initiates who are genuinely tired of spiritual half-measures, and are prepared to undertake serious hardships in order to make great spiritual advancements.

+ Constantine

OPENING THE BLACK CORRIDOR

1. Gather a sharp knife, three black candles, and some ashes mixed with urine and earth (in a small bowl).
2. Go to an isolated room.
3. Cut the left hand, preferably the ring finger. Dribble the blood into the bowl, mix into the ashes and urine, so that it forms a muddy paste.
4. Taking the ashen paste, and trace a circle on the ground. It does not need to be perfect or even very neat, but it should be large enough to sit in.
5. Place the three black candles along the circle at intervals.
6. Light the candles.
7. Whisper (first candle): *NOMEN*, then (second candle): *ANIMA*, then (third candle): *CORPUS*.
8. Extinguish all light in the room. Seat yourself in the circle.
9. Cut the hand again, so that blood flows liberally over the thumb and fingers.
10. With bloody fingers, extinguish the first candle. Intone the secret name of the Abyss, internally.
11. With bloody fingers, extinguish the second candle. Intone the secret name of the Abyss, internally.
12. With bloody fingers, extinguish the third candle. Intone the secret name of the Abyss, internally.

13. Sitting now in the darkness, in the middle of the circle, you need to call out to the very spirit of the Abyss. *This cannot be done with words*, it can only be done through silent keening. Your very spirit needs to wail, loudly and mournfully. If you can do this with sincerity, the Abyss will hear you.

14. Open yourself to the spirits, which are drawn to the location. The ritual itself will open a corridor to the Abyss, even if only briefly. Be prepared to accept whatever spirit is released, which will likely expect to be hosted within you.

15. Wait within the triangle until contact is achieved. It is normal to experience fear or anxiety during the ritual.

16. Once contact with the Abyss (or Abyssal spirit) is accomplished, then leave the chamber. Do not attempt a banishing,

It would be very normal for poltergeist phenomena to occur during and after the ritual. The spirits that are attracted by this ritual are nearly impossible to banish by normal occult means, so the adept who performs this ritual should be prepared for long-term effects.

ARTISTS PORTFOLIOS ONLINE

VLF

www.vlfvideo.blogspot.com

Edgar Kerval

www.sunbehindthesun.blogspot.com

Nestoe Avalos

nestoravalosofficialblackartssit.tumblr.com/

Erica Frevel

cargocollective.com/EricaFrevel

Joel Hrafnsson

serpentshrinesinistra.wordpress.com

ATU III

www.ingramcontent.com/pod-product-compliance
Lightning Source LLC
LaVergne TN
LVHW061304060426
835511LV00015B/2075